LAODICEA

JACK SEQUEIRA

LAODICEA

*Christ's urgent counsel
to a lukewarm church
in the last days*

Jack Sequeira

Pacific Press Publishing Association
Boise, Idaho
Oshawa, Ontario, Canada

Edited by B. Russell Holt
Designed by Dennis Ferree
Cover illustration by Lori Anzalone
Typeset in 12/15 Jansen

Copyright © 1995 by
Pacific Press Publishing Association
Printed in the United States of America
All Rights Reserved

Library of Congress Cataloging-in-Publication Data

Sequeira, Jack.
    Laodicea : Christ's urgent counsel to a lukewarm church in the last days / Jack Sequeira.
       p.   cm.
    Includes bibliographical references.
    ISBN 0-8163-1243-5
    1. Bible. N. T. Revelation III, 14-22—Criticism, interpretation, etc. 2. Christian life—Seventh-day Adventist authors. 3. Christian life—Adventist authors. 4. Christian life—Sabbatarian authors. I. Title.
BS2825.2.S48   1995
228'.06—dc20
                                                  94-33495
                                                           CIP

95 96 97 98 99 • 5 4 3 2

Contents

Preface 7

Introduction 9

Chapter 1
Laodicea is addressed 17

Chapter 2
Laodicea is evaluated—I 29

Chapter 3
Laodicea is evaluated—II 41

Chapter 4
Laodicea is deceived 51

Chapter 5
Laodicea is counseled 63

Chapter 6
Laodicea is rebuked 75

Chapter 7
Laodicea must repent 87

Chapter 8
Laodicea must open the door 99

Chapter 9
Laodicea must overcome 113

Chapter 10
Laodicea is sealed 123

Chapter 11
Laodicea is faultless 135

Preface

Seventh-day Adventists have long had difficulty dealing with the message to Laodicea recorded in Revelation 3:14-22. In the months and years following the Great Disappointment of 1844, Sabbath-keeping Adventists rather smugly applied this message to those Adventists who had not accepted the seventh-day Sabbath or the changing ministry of Christ in the heavenly sanctuary.

Thus in 1865, when Ellen White—as a result of divine enlightenment—began applying the Laodicean message to her fellow Sabbatarian Adventists, they greeted her words with shocked dismay. Serious introspection led many to recognize the truthfulness of the application. Spiritual revival followed.

Soon, however, the drive to perfect church organization and the strains of the American Civil War preoccupied most Seventh-day Adventists. The concept that the counsel to Laodicea applied to them became an accepted, but strangely neglected, doctrine. Yet the Laodicean message itself requires not only belief, but action.

There was plenty of action among Seventh-day Adventists during the remaining years of the nineteenth century. This action brought a great increase in evangelism, but tragically, it also brought a great increase in internal dispute. In spite of the attention given to the importance of the idea of righteousness by faith that developed in 1888 and during the years that followed, most Adventists found it

LAODICEA

difficult to accept the True Witness's evaluation of Laodicea and apply His counsel to themselves.

This condition has persisted to the present. Even with repeated calls for revival and reformation, we have continued in a lukewarm state. A lukewarm bath can be comfortable and relaxing. So can the conviction that we have "the truth" and the knowledge that we are experiencing dramatic growth in church membership. But Christ has not found a lukewarm church appealing. Rather, He finds it nauseating. And so Pastor Jack Sequeira, through careful and convincing biblical exposition, seeks to arouse us to our true condition—and to acceptance of the gracious remedy provided. He does not pretend that this will be easy for us, *but it is essential.*

In the end, the Laodicean message is one that inspires hope and enthusiasm. Hope for ourselves and enthusiasm over the marvelous opportunity to bring glory to our loving heavenly Father and to our gracious Redeemer through the power of His indwelling Spirit.

Pastor Sequeira's earnest desire is to help us sing—and practice—with honesty and humility that old gospel song, "Not I, but Christ." As that chorus swells from an ever-increasing number of Jesus' followers, they will overcome even as He overcame and accept His kind invitation to join Him in His throne (see Revelation 3:21). May that day be soon!

Richard W. Schwartz
Professor of History, Emeritus
Andrews University

Introduction

The book of Revelation is primarily the prophetic history of the body of Christ, the church, which God revealed to His Son to be shared with His people through the apostle John. Although it had meaning for John's first-century readers, it has special significance to Christians living in these last days. It reveals "things which must shortly come to pass" (Revelation 1:1). It promises a special blessing to those who read and pay attention to its message (see verse 3). Yet it is written in highly symbolic language, so that to recover its hidden treasure requires much digging. That is what we intend to do in this book concerning the end-time church so that we may understand and appreciate the present truth in Christ's message to Laodicea.

Before we get into the message to the Laodicean church, we need to understand some things about the book of Revelation as a whole. Revelation complements the Old Testament book of Daniel. Both books focus primarily on last-day events. In fact, many of the symbols John uses in Revelation come from Daniel's book. For example, when we read in Revelation 14:8, "Babylon is fallen, is fallen, that great city," we need to understand that John is making a spiritual application of the destruction of the historical city of Babylon as described in Daniel, chapter 5.

How shall we interpret the symbols in these two books? Today, there are primarily four methods of interpreting Daniel and Revelation.

LAODICEA

The historicist method. The Reformers believed that both Daniel and Revelation reveal the history of the world and of the Christian church, beginning at the times of the writers and continuing to the end of the world. In this view, Daniel and John began with their own contemporary time (about 600 B.C. for Daniel and about A.D. 100 for John) and gave a continuous account of historical events culminating with the last days. Thus for the Reformers, the little horn of Daniel 7 and 8 represented pagan and papal Rome, and the antichrist of Revelation symbolized the papacy. Naturally, Roman Catholic scholars didn't agree with this historicist method of interpretation. To counter it, they developed two alternatives—the preterist and the futurist methods.

The preterist method. This view teaches that all the prophecies of Daniel and Revelation were fulfilled within a very short period following the time of the writer—by the second century B.C. for Daniel and by the third century A.D. for Revelation. Obviously, if such a view is correct, the papacy cannot be included in these prophecies. So the preterist method allowed the Catholic Church to avoid being identified as the little horn of Daniel or the antichrist of Revelation. According to this view, these symbols refer to such long-ago powers as Antiochus Ephiphanes and the Roman Empire.

The futurist method. Roman Catholic scholars also developed a second method of interpreting Daniel and Revelation that exempts the papacy as a fulfillment of the symbols in these books. The futurist view teaches that some of Daniel's and John's prophecies were fulfilled in the time of the writers and that others will be fulfilled in the future at the very end of the church's history. Between these two periods is a long gap of time that is not covered at all by the prophecies of Daniel or Revelation. And, of course, this in-between period includes the history of the Roman Catholic Church.

The idealistic method. Liberal theologians originated this view, but some conservative Christians are beginning to accept it as well. It teaches that the prophecies of Daniel and Revelation aren't really

Introduction

prophecies of actual events at all; they are simply symbols that reveal spiritual truths. Instead of pointing to any specific point in history, these "prophecies" are symbolic of general spiritual themes that have repeated themselves over and over again in the course of this world's history—and will continue to do so.

So these are the four methods of interpreting Daniel and Revelation currently in use today. It's easy to understand why Roman Catholics would use the preterist and futurist methods in order to defend their church against the historicist viewpoint. But amazingly enough, the Protestant churches have gradually adopted these preterist and futurist methods as well! Most Protestants today are either preterists or futurists in their interpretation of Daniel and Revelation.

For example, many Protestants interpret the seventy weeks of Daniel 9 using the gap theory of the futurist method. They say that the first sixty-nine weeks were fulfilled in Daniel's day and that the seventieth week will be fulfilled at the end of time. Thus they place a long gap of time between the first sixty-nine weeks and the final, seventieth one. Those who teach a "secret rapture" and those who are dispensationalists both follow this gap theory of the futurist method.

The result is that there is hardly any Christian denomination today, except the Seventh-day Adventist, which continues to teach the historicist view of interpreting the prophecies of Daniel and Revelation. Seventh-day Adventists stand virtually alone in upholding the Reformation understanding of these two books. Yet if we are concerned to emphasize God's all-knowing understanding of earth's history, the historicist interpretation is the one that makes the most sense. I believe that this method, the one the Reformers proclaimed, is the correct method. This is the method we will use in this book to interpret Christ's message to the Laodicean church.

We also need to keep in mind another principle of interpretation when we are studying the books of Daniel and Revelation—the principle of parallelism or recapitulation. This means that these books not

LAODICEA

only outline the history of the world and especially of the church; they do so repeatedly from different angles. For example, Daniel chapters 2, 7, and 8 are parallel passages; they each cover the same period of history, but each emphasizes different details. Revelation does the same thing using the theme of sevens. There are the seven churches, the seven seals, the seven trumpets, etc. All these parallel passages deal with the same time periods, but each concentrates on a different issue.

Therefore, we must consider the context of all seven of the churches (Revelation 1-3) in order to accurately understand what Christ is saying to the Laodicean church, the last in the series. We need to ask, "What is Christ trying to get across in His messages to these seven churches? Is there something that ties them all together?"

There is, and when we look at Christ's message to each of these churches, we find what it is. To the first church, Ephesus, Christ says, "I know thy works" (Revelation 2:2). And He repeats this same phrase to each of the seven churches in turn. To the church of Smyrna, He says, "I know thy works" (verse 9). This phrase is the common thread that links each church with the others. To each, Jesus says, "I know thy works"—Pergamos (verse 13), Thyatira (verse 19), Sardis (Revelation 3:1), Philadelphia (verse 8), and Laodicea (verse 15).

Based on this common phrase, what is Christ doing in His messages to the seven churches? He is evaluating their spiritual condition. You see, God judges churches and individuals by their works. This is clear New Testament teaching. "By their fruits ye shall know them" (Matthew 7:20). Our works reveal our spiritual condition. So the messages to the seven churches are Christ's evaluation of the spiritual condition of His people from John's day right up to the last generation.

The New Testament is clear that our works reveal our spiritual condition. In Matthew 5:14, 16, Jesus told His disciples, "Ye [plural] are the light [singular] of the world. . . . Let your light so shine before men, that they may see your good works, and glorify your Father which is in heaven." Christ is *the* light, but we who are His body are to repre-

Introduction

sent Him to the world by our good works. Our works reveal whether or not we are truly reflecting the Saviour.

When Jesus comes, He will divide the world into two groups—the sheep and the goats. Although no one is saved by his or her works, Jesus says to the sheep, "I was hungry, and you fed me. I was naked, and you clothed me. I was sick, and you visited me" (see Matthew 25:33-36). Justification by faith always bears fruit, and the fruit it bears is good works. Here, Jesus is pointing to the good works of His followers as evidence that they have accepted His righteousness. Likewise, He points to the absence of good works as the evidence that the goats have rejected His salvation (see verses 41-46).

Another Bible example of how our works reveal our spiritual condition is found in James's letter. He says, "Wilt thou know, O vain man, that faith without works is dead?" (James 2:20). It appears on the surface that James is teaching justification by works. But if you read what he says carefully, you will find that he is defending the idea that genuine justification by faith will always produce good works. To those who say, "Thou hast faith, and I have works," James replies, "Shew me thy faith without thy works, and I will shew thee my faith by my works" (verse 18). Faith and works, James argues, cannot be separated. And Paul agrees with him. What is the evidence of our faith? Not merely our words, but also the revelation of God's power in our lives (see 1 Corinthians 4:20). The world isn't impressed by Christians who shout and lift up their hands and say, "Praise the Lord, I am saved!" The world wants to see Christ and His power working in our lives. The philosopher Friedrich Nietzsche once challenged the Christian church, "If you expect me to believe in your redeemer, you Christians will have to look a lot more redeemed!"

So when Jesus tells each of the seven churches, "I know thy works," He is simply saying, "I'm evaluating your spiritual condition. Are your works good? Are they bad? What is your condition?" This is the common thread running through each of His messages to the seven

LAODICEA

churches. The True Witness evaluates each church.

We will also find as we examine the messages to these churches that each follows a pattern made up of four basic elements:

1. Commendation. Jesus makes note of the good points about each church.

2. Reproof. Judging each church by its works, Jesus says, "This is what I have against you."

3. Counsel. Jesus never rebukes His church without giving it a remedy for its problems. For every problem the church faces, there is counsel.

4. Promise. Jesus closes His counsel with a promise. If His people will accept the counsel and follow it, the promise will be fulfilled to them.

But there are some interesting exceptions to this pattern. Jesus has no reproof for two of the seven churches—Smyrna and Philadelphia. Unfortunately, He has much to say in reproof to Laodicea, the church representing the time in which we live.

But there is something even more disturbing about Christ's message to Laodicea than His reproof. Not only does Jesus reprove Laodicea, *He has nothing good to say about her!* There is no commendation for the Laodicean church. Ellen White says, "The message to the church of the Laodiceans is a startling denunciation, and is applicable to the people of God at the present time" (*Testimonies for the Church*, 3:252).

Here is a church that claims to have present truth—and Jesus has no commendation for her! Here is a church that claims to be God's remnant church—and Christ says, "I have nothing good to say about you!" That certainly is a startling denunciation!

Where have we gone wrong? What is our problem? We must look at Christ's message to Laodicea honestly. We need to go to the Word of God to discover what He is saying to us. But first note how Ellen White applies this message to the Seventh-day Adventist Church:

Introduction

The message to the Laodicean church is highly applicable to us as a people. It has been placed before us for a long time, but has not been heeded as it should have been. When the work of repentance is most earnest and deep, the individual members of the church will buy the rich goods of heaven (*SDA Bible Commentary*, 7:961).

I was shown that the testimony to the Laodiceans applies to God's people at the present time, and the reason it has not accomplished a greater work is because of the hardness of their hearts (*Testimonies for the Church*, 1:186).

The Laodicean message applies to the people of God who profess to believe present truth. The greater part are lukewarm professors, having a name but no zeal (ibid., 4:87).

As already stated, Revelation is a book of symbols. But we cannot use a dictionary or our culture to interpret these symbols. We must go to Scripture itself. When Jesus says to us, "You are not hot or cold, but lukewarm" (see Revelation 3:15, 16), we must go to the Bible and ask, What does Scripture mean by these terms—*hot, cold,* and *lukewarm?*

As we will see, Jesus uses a different, special name for Himself when He speaks to each of the seven churches, a name that is connected with the message to that particular church. When He speaks to Laodicea, He calls Himself the "Amen" (see verse 14). What does He mean by that? What does it say about Him? He also calls Himself "the faithful and true witness" and "the beginning [or source] of the creation of God" (verse 14). Why does He refer to Himself by these three titles when speaking to Laodicea? What relationship do they have to His message to us and to our spiritual condition? These are questions that we must come to grips with if we expect to understand what Christ is saying to the Laodicean church.

LAODICEA

In the message to Laodicea, we are dealing with God's evaluation of the last generation of Christians. In a very specific way, we are dealing with God's evaluation of the Seventh-day Adventist Church. Is it a good evaluation? A bad evaluation? Is there anything about the church that God can commend? No. Is there any reproof for the church? Yes, there certainly is. Does this reproof apply only to a few members, or does it apply to the whole community of believers? Does it include you? Does it include me?

Further, Christ's message to Laodicea is vitally connected with the message of righteousness by faith—the message God brought to this church in 1888. We will see this connection from the Bible itself as we study Christ's words to the church of Laodicea—your church and mine. This is clearly supported by Ellen White. "The Laodicean message has been sounding. Take this message in all its phases and sound it forth to the people wherever Providence opens the way. Justification by faith and the righteousness of Christ are the themes to be presented to a perishing world" (*SDA Bible Commentary*, 7:964). This message is one that we first need to apply to ourselves before we attempt to share it with others. When we see ourselves in Christ's description of Laodicea—poor, naked, and blind—then we can take the message of life to a world that is dying. This message will illuminate the entire world with God's glory, but it must first illuminate our own lives with the righteousness of Jesus.

That is the purpose of this book. In this message to the church of Laodicea, Christ is speaking to you and me. When we understand and apply His words to ourselves, they will bring revival and power to our lives.

CHAPTER 1

LAODICEA
is addressed

Unto the angel of the church of the Laodiceans write; These things saith the Amen, the faithful and true witness, the beginning of the creation of God.
REVELATION 3:14

When we write a letter, we identify the person to whom we are writing in a greeting—"Dear Mary," or "Dear John." And we sign our name to show who has written the letter. Just so, Revelation 3:14, the introduction to Jesus' letter to Laodicea, contains these same two items. It identifies the one to whom this letter is addressed, and it names the One who is sending it—the recipient and the Sender.

If you will look carefully at verse 14, you'll notice that the letter to Laodicea is addressed, not to the church itself, but to the "angel" of the church. This is true, also, of each of the letters to the seven churches. Each is actually addressed to the "angel" of that church. What does this mean? Who is this "angel"?

To answer these questions, we need to go back to Revelation, chapter 1 and look at the introduction to these messages to the seven

LAODICEA

churches. In chapter 1, we find John in vision on "the Lord's day" (verse 10). He hears a voice and turns to see who is speaking to him. The first thing he sees in vision are seven golden candlesticks. And in the middle of these candlesticks, or lampstands, he sees "one like unto the Son of man" (verse 13). This is Jesus Christ. While He was here on earth, Jesus commonly referred to Himself as the "Son of man." He called Himself by this title in order to identify Himself with us.

So John hears Jesus and sees Him walking among the golden candlesticks. In his vision, John sees Jesus holding "in his right hand seven stars: and out of his mouth went a sharp twoedged sword" (verse 16). The New Testament symbolizes the Bible, God's Word, as a sharp two-edged sword (see Hebrews 4:12).

Verse 20 explains the symbols of the seven golden candlesticks and the seven stars in Jesus' right hand: "The seven stars," Jesus tells John, "are the angels of the seven churches: and the seven candlesticks which thou sawest are the seven churches."

The seven candlesticks represent the churches themselves. This is an appropriate symbol. In His Sermon on the Mount, Jesus said to His followers, "Ye are the light of the world" (Matthew 5:14). But in John 8:12, Jesus said of Himself, "I am the light of the world." Which is it? Are we Christians the world's light, or is Jesus? How can both statements be true?

The answer is evident in the original language of Matthew 5:14. It isn't so apparent in English, but in Greek it is clear that the word *ye* is plural; Jesus is referring to all Christians. But the word *light* is singular. There is only one light, and that light is Jesus Christ. He is "the true Light, which lighteth every man that cometh into the world" (John 1:9). So when Jesus said in Matthew 5:14, "Ye [all His people] are the light [Christ's representatives] of the world," He was saying that His church is to reflect Him, the true light of the world. The church is to represent Christ to the world. The world needs to see "Christ in you, the hope of glory" (Colossians 1:27). Whatever light we shed in the

Laodicea is addressed

world is the result of reflecting the rays from the true Light, Jesus Christ.

Jesus went on to say that when a person lights a candle, he puts it on a candlestick so that it will give light to everyone around. That, He said, is how His people are to shine for Him in this dark world (see Matthew 5:15, 16). Like candles set on a candlestick, each member of God's church is to let his light (Christ in you) so shine before men that they may see his good works and glorify the Father who is in heaven. So the symbol of seven candlesticks representing the seven churches is very fitting. We need to keep this in mind as we look at Christ's message to Laodicea in order to understand why the church has failed to be the light of the world that God intended her to be.

It's clear, then, that when John saw in vision Jesus walking among seven candlesticks, holding seven stars in His right hand, the candlesticks represent the seven churches (see Revelation 1:20). But who or what do the stars in Jesus' hand represent?

Verse 20 clearly answers that question also: "The seven stars are the angels of the seven churches." Remember that each of Christ's letters to the seven churches is addressed to the "angel" of that church. What does this symbolize?

The word *angel* means "messenger." Hebrews 1:14 describes angels as "ministering spirits, sent forth to minister for them who shall be heirs of salvation." They are God's messengers to minister to us who are the recipients of salvation. So when Jesus speaks of the "angel" of each of the seven churches, He is referring to those who are the spiritual leaders of the church. The Living Bible paraphrase doesn't use the word *angel* in these verses in Revelation that speak of the seven churches. It uses the word *leader*. That's the correct sense of the word; the "angel" of the Laodicean church symbolizes the "spiritual leader" of that church.

A church's spiritual leaders include the elders, Sabbath School teachers, and other officers. But the primary meaning seems to refer

LAODICEA

to the pastor, the shepherd who is in charge of the spiritual condition of the church. Ellen White says:

> God's ministers are symbolized by the seven stars, which He who is the first and the last [Christ] has under His special care and protection. The sweet influences that are to be abundant in the church are bound up with these ministers of God, who are to represent the love of Christ. The stars of heaven are under God's control. He fills them with light. He guides and directs their movements. If He did not, they would become fallen stars (*Gospel Workers*, 13, 14).

To a large degree, the spiritual condition of the church is in the hands of the ministers. Traveling to Jerusalem from his missionary journeys, Paul stopped briefly in Miletus, where he met with the leaders of the church in Ephesus. He challenged them, "Take heed therefore unto yourselves, and to all the flock, over which the Holy Ghost hath made you overseers, to feed the church of God, which he hath purchased with his own blood" (Acts 20:28). We have placed many responsibilities on our pastors today, but their primary task is to feed the church spiritually and bring about growth in grace. The spiritual condition of the church will depend largely on the pastor and the food with which he feeds his flock every Sabbath.

All of us, when we first believe in Christ and accept His gift of salvation, do so from a selfish motive. There may be rare exceptions. But because our human natures are selfish, we usually accept Christ in the beginning because we are afraid of punishment or because we want the reward. Our evangelism often appeals to these same motives. When we tell people that there is "a heaven to gain and a hell to shun," aren't we appealing to their egocentric natures? Of course, it's true that we should want to gain heaven and shun hell. But if that is the only motivation, then we are operating from basically a selfish orientation.

Laodicea is addressed

Quite honestly, both my wife and I joined the Seventh-day Adventist Church out of fear! We were both scared of the investigative judgment that we were told about in evangelistic meetings. They were not the same meetings; we lived eight thousand miles apart at that time, but Adventist evangelistic meetings are much the same the world over. So we listened to the same twenty-five subjects, and we made our decisions based on fear—on what would happen to us if we didn't choose to accept. Such a decision may be better than no decision at all, but fear (or the hope of reward) is a poor motive upon which to base your spiritual life!

Likewise, the disciples—all twelve of them—accepted Jesus for selfish reasons. Even after three years spent with Jesus, what were they arguing about in the upper room? They were arguing about who would be the most important in the coming kingdom! They were still thinking of themselves.

So, like my wife and me, like the disciples, most of us are what Paul calls "carnal" Christians, or "babes in Christ" (1 Corinthians 3:1), when we first accept Jesus and join His church. It's the pastor's responsibility to feed these spiritual babies so they will grow. As the spiritual leader of the church, he is to help them move from carnality to spirituality. There has to be spiritual growth. A carnal Christian is a weak Christian, a baby in Christ, and the pastor must carefully nourish him and help him to grow.

In His letter to the Laodicean church, Christ is saying, "Pastors, there is something wrong with the church." Of course, the message to Laodicea is relevant to every member of the church (see Revelation 1:11), but the ministers have a special responsibility to build up the church. We need to pray for our ministers and pastors, that they will feed the flock and help it to grow spiritually. Ellen White recognized the special importance of Jesus' words to church leaders: " 'These things saith he that holdeth the seven stars in his right hand.' These words are spoken to the teachers in the church—those entrusted by God

LAODICEA

with weighty responsibilities" (*Review and Herald*, 26 May 1903).

So now we have seen to whom in Laodicea Jesus has addressed His letter. He addresses it to the ministers, the spiritual leaders of the church. Yet Jesus is not speaking only to them; He isn't addressing just certain individuals in the church. Through the leaders, He is speaking to the whole church, to every member. There is something dreadfully wrong with the Laodicean church, and Christ is appealing to the leadership of the church—and through them to every member—to realize the urgency of what He is saying. The whole church, top to bottom, needs to understand this message, and the leaders, particularly, must consider it carefully.

Now let's look at the second half of Revelation 3:14. What names does Jesus use when He "signs" the letter to the Laodicean church?

In every one of the seven letters to the churches, Jesus gives Himself a special title, or name. And in each case the title He gives Himself harmonizes with the special needs of that church. Therefore, the title Christ gives Himself when speaking to Laodicea is based on Laodicea's needs; it is connected with the message to that church. Here is what Jesus calls Himself when He is speaking to Laodicea: "These things saith the Amen, the faithful and true witness, the beginning of the creation of God" (Revelation 3:14).

First, Jesus refers to Himself as the "Amen, the faithful and true witness." The word *Amen* is being used here as a proper noun, a name. *Amen* actually means "so be it." Or it can mean "the truth," or "what is being said is the truth." The emphasis in this first title seems to be on the truthfulness of Jesus' witness to Laodicea.

Why does He need to stress the truthfulness, the accuracy, of what He is saying? Because, as we will see in more detail later, there is a great discrepancy between Laodicea's evaluation of herself and the evaluation that Christ gives. Laodicea has a major problem: her self-evaluation does not agree with Christ's evaluation of her spiritual condition. Laodicea says, "I am rich, and increased with goods, and

Laodicea is addressed

have need of nothing." Jesus says, "Thou art wretched, and miserable, and poor, and blind, and naked" (Revelation 3:17).

Who says that Laodicea is wretched, miserable, poor, blind, and naked? Jesus Christ, "the Amen, the faithful and true witness" (verse 14). Yet we Laodiceans deny this. We claim the very opposite to be true. We say that we are rich and increased with goods and need nothing. Do these two evaluations agree? Clearly not. Therefore, the question is: Who is right? Obviously, the Faithful and True Witness is right. That's what Jesus wants to emphasize. That's why He calls Himself "the Amen," the truth, the Faithful and True Witness.

We need to clearly understand that the church is the body of Christ. It's a corporate whole—a *koinonia*—made up of individual members, just as is the physical body. When a person's hand is diseased, the whole body is affected—not just the hand. The Bible is clear on this point. For example, when Daniel prayed (Daniel 9), he said, "*We* have sinned against thee" (verse 8, emphasis supplied). He included himself in the sins of Israel that had brought them into captivity in Babylon. Was this true of Daniel personally? No. Yet he identified himself with God's people. He understood that the church is a corporate body and that what affects one affects all.

This is my main complaint against many of the independent movements that are arising these days to criticize the church: They hold up the shortcomings of the church, and then they look upon themselves in self-righteousness as if they alone are on the right track. The Bible teaches that we are all one body; we each need to identify ourselves with the mistakes of the church, for we are one. I might look at myself and say, "I'm all right; I'm feeding the people in my sermons and writings. I'm doing my job." But the truth is that I, too, am part of the body and thus part of the problem that Christ identifies in Laodicea.

We in Laodicea today have the same problem Peter had. Just before His betrayal, Jesus sadly announced, "All ye shall be offended because of me this night: for it is written, I will smite the shepherd, and the

LAODICEA

sheep of the flock shall be scattered abroad" (Matthew 26:31). All the disciples denied it, and Peter denied it vehemently.

"Though all men shall be offended because of thee," Peter replied, "yet will I never be offended" (verse 33).

Jesus said to Peter, "Verily I say unto thee, That this night, before the cock crow, thou shalt deny me thrice" (verse 34).

But Peter insisted, "Though I should die with thee, yet will I not deny thee" (verse 35).

Peter had the Laodicean problem. Jesus had one evaluation of him. Peter had another, far different, evaluation of himself. Did they agree? No. Who was right? Jesus was right. Just think how much embarrassment and how many problems Peter would have avoided if he had simply said, "Yes, Lord, You know all things. You are right, and I am wrong." But Peter had to learn the hard way that Jesus knew him better than he knew himself. That Jesus' evaluation was the truth.

In His letter to the Laodicean church, Jesus is saying, "I am the True Witness. What I am telling you is the truth. You may not agree with Me, but I am telling you the truth. You may not like to hear it, but I'm telling you the truth." And if we don't learn to listen to Christ now, like Peter, we will have to learn the hard way, for Jesus warns, "If you don't repent, I will rebuke you and spew you out of My mouth" (see Revelation 3:16).

Jesus also calls Himself by a second name, or title, in His letter to the Laodicean church. He refers to Himself as "the beginning of the creation of God" (verse 14). This title, especially as it is given in the King James Version of the Bible, has caused a lot of problems. Many Christians through the years, including some Seventh-day Adventist pioneers, have understood Jesus to be saying that somewhere back in the past ages, He had a beginning as the first being God created. One early Adventist writer tried to minimize this difficulty by saying that Christ's origin was so far back in the days of eternity that as far as humans were concerned, it was almost as though Christ really didn't have a beginning. Ellen White, however, took an opposite view. In her book *The Desire of Ages*, she wrote: "In Christ is life, original, unborrowed, underived" (530). Thus she took a position that was contrary to the thinking of most of the early leaders of the Seventh-day Adventist Church. And her view was in harmony with the clear teaching of the New Testament.

You see, when Christ calls Himself "the beginning of the creation of God," He isn't saying that He was the first being God created and that He hadn't existed before that time. The word *beginning* here simply means "the source" or "the origin" or "the chief cause." Christ is saying, "I am the Source of all creation."

This is what the New Testament teaches clearly. "All things were made by him [Christ]; and without him was not any thing made that was made" (John 1:3). Speaking of Jesus, Paul says, "By him were all things created, that are in heaven, and that are in earth. . . . He is before all things, and by him all things consist" (Colossians 1:16, 17; see also 1 Corinthians 8:6; Ephesians 3:9). Jesus is saying to the Laodiceans, "I am not only the True Witness, I am also the Source of all creation. I can re-create you into My image, but only if you allow Me to do so. I can create in you a new heart; I can make you a new person, but only if you repent and accept My true evaluation of you."

He is not only saying, "I am telling you the truth about yourselves, as painful as that may be." He is also saying, "I am the solution to your problems." That is why He calls Himself by two titles. "I am the Faithful and True Witness," He says, "because you need to know your true condition. You aren't even aware of it; you are in denial regarding it, so you need the truth." And then He says, "But I have the solution to your problem. I am the Source of God's creation. I made everything, and I can re-create your heart."

In reality, Jesus is offering to fulfill in us the new covenant promise. He made this promise first to the Jewish nation, but the Jews rejected Him. What was the result? With tears in His eyes and tears in His

LAODICEA

voice, Jesus looked out over Jerusalem during His triumphal entry into the city just before His crucifixion, saying, "O Jerusalem, Jerusalem . . . how often would I have gathered thy children together, even as a hen gathereth her chickens under her wings, and ye would not!" (Matthew 23:37). In other words, "I am going to spew you out of My mouth as a nation, and I will turn to the Gentiles."

Christ couldn't fulfill the new covenant promises to the Jewish nation because it had made its ultimate and irrevocable decision to reject Him. Individual Jews could still take advantage of the promises, of course, but the nation as a whole had turned away. Now He is making the same new covenant promises to us today. The original promises found in Ezekiel 11:19, 20; 36:26, 27 are repeated to us in Hebrews 8:10-13.

So what have we discovered as we have examined the opening address of Christ's letter to the Laodicean church?

We have learned that Christ is not speaking only to a few people in the church. He is addressing the leadership, but through the leaders, He is speaking to the entire membership. The problems Jesus points out in Laodicea are not the problems of only a few of its members. They are the problems of the whole corporate body of Christ, the last generation of Christians, and they apply especially to the Seventh-day Adventist Church.

We have learned that although Christ's spiritual evaluation of us is negative, it is nevertheless true. The question for us becomes: "Are we willing to accept His evaluation of our lives, painful though it is?" It's painful when someone says to us, "You are wretched, miserable, poor, blind, and naked"—especially when we are a church that claims to have the truth. It is very painful. But if we are going to experience Christ's solution to our problems, we are going to have to accept what the True Witness is saying about us. Let's not apply this message to other churches; let's apply it first to ourselves.

We have been deceived regarding our own spirituality, just as the

Laodicea is addressed

Jews were deceived regarding their experience with God. "The heart is deceitful above all things, and desperately wicked: who can know it?" (Jeremiah 17:9). The Jews rejected Christ because they did not accept His evaluation of them. We must not do the same.

When we look at Christ's evaluation of us in the letter to the Laodiceans, we will have to make a response: Is it true? Is it false? If we decide it is true, then we will take His counsel. If we decide it is false, then we will refuse the counsel and will be spewed out of His mouth. Thus the words of Jesus to Laodicea become vitally important to us.

What is our problem as identified by the Faithful and True Witness? What is it that we don't know? What is it that has deceived us? What does Jesus mean when He says that our works are neither hot nor cold, but lukewarm? Does He mean that we aren't doing enough works? I don't think that is true. We are not lacking works, but our works have a problem. What is wrong with our works?

These are questions we will be considering in the next chapter.

CHAPTER 2

LAODICEA
is evaluated—I

I know thy works, that thou art neither cold nor hot: I would thou wert cold or hot. So then because thou art lukewarm, and neither cold nor hot, I will spue thee out of my mouth.
REVELATION 3:15, 16

These two verses are the key to Christ's entire message to Laodicea. They are its most important section, and if we want to understand what He is telling us in this letter, we must clearly understand what He is saying in these two verses. The reason they are so important is that these two verses are Christ's evaluation of Laodicea's spiritual condition. All the rest of His letter is based on that evaluation. Because this evaluation is so important, we will spend this chapter and the next examining it.

The Faithful and True Witness begins His evaluation of Laodicea by saying, "I know thy works" (verse 15). What does He mean?

Jesus is not talking about our denominational activities; He isn't referring to our hospitals, colleges, publishing houses, orphanages, or nursing homes. He is talking about our spiritual works collectively as well as our individual lives—our behavior, our actions. If our spiritual

LAODICEA

behavior as a people is wrong, then our institutional works will naturally be affected also. They may be just a fair showing of the flesh. What does the True Witness say about our works? How does He evaluate them?

First, we need to recognize that Laodicea is not lacking in works. Christ makes that clear when He assures us, "I know thy works" (verse 15). The issue is not that we don't demonstrate enough works. We have plenty of works, but there is something wrong with them. What is the problem with our works?

According to the Faithful and True Witness, the problem with our works is that they are neither hot nor cold, but lukewarm. That is the evaluation He gives. Notice that Christ's words allow for three kinds of works: hot works, cold works, and lukewarm works. What does Jesus mean by hot works? By cold works? By lukewarm works?

Remember that the book of Revelation is written in symbols that must be defined by the Word of God as a whole. If we look carefully at the New Testament, we will discover that it describes human spiritual behavior—our works—in three categories. These three types of works are: works of the flesh, works of faith, and works of law. I believe these correspond to Christ's reference to cold works, hot works, and lukewarm works in His message to Laodicea. If we are going to understand what Jesus is saying, we need to understand what each of these kinds of works is and why He refers to them as He does.

I would suggest that when Jesus speaks of "cold works," He is referring to what the New Testament calls "works of the flesh." Paul says, "I am carnal [fleshly], sold under sin" (Romans 7:14). He means, "I am a fallen, sinful man." The New Testament consistently uses the word *flesh* in a spiritual sense to refer to our fallen, sinful natures. So works of the flesh are the sins we commit, our sinful behavior. Paul clearly describes them: "Now the works of the flesh are manifest, which are these; Adultery, fornication, uncleanness, lasciviousness, idolatry, witchcraft, hatred, variance, emulations, wrath, strife, seditions, heresies, envyings, murders, drunkenness, revellings, and such like" (Galatians 5:19-21). If we were to describe the works of the flesh in one word, it would be *sin!*

Paul reinforces this point in Romans 7. He says, "I know that in me (that is, in my flesh,) dwelleth no good thing: for to will is present with me; but how to perform that which is good I find not" (verse 18). Paul is saying that his flesh, that is, his sinful nature, is incapable of doing good because of the sin that lives there. "I delight in the law of God after the inward man," he continues, "but I see another law in my members, warring against the law of my mind, and bringing me into captivity to the law of sin which is in my members [flesh]. . . . So then with the mind I myself serve the law of God; but with the flesh the law of sin" (verses 22, 23, 25). The apostle admits that left on his own, without the help of the Holy Spirit, all he can do is to acknowledge in his mind that God's law is good, but in his flesh (sinful nature) he is a slave to sin. This is why Paul reminds the Christians in Rome, "There is none righteous, no, not one. . . . There is none that doeth good, no, not one" (Romans 3:10, 12).

That is why Paul declares, "The carnal [fleshly] mind is enmity against God: for it is not subject to the law of God, neither indeed can be" (Romans 8:7). In other words, the flesh can do nothing good. Jesus said to Nicodemus, "That which is born of the flesh is flesh" (John 3:6). The flesh is unchangeable. Jesus is telling Nicodemus, "Your foundation is all wrong. You are trying to do the will of God by the flesh. But the flesh will always remain sinful. You need to be born from above; you need to have another power, the power of the Holy Spirit, within you."

Why should we identify "works of the flesh" or sinful acts with the "cold works" Jesus speaks about in His message to Laodicea? In Matthew 24, Jesus is prophesying about conditions in the last days, the days in which you and I are living. He says, "Because iniquity shall abound, the love of many shall wax cold" (verse 12). Here, Jesus iden-

LAODICEA

tifies the word *cold* with iniquity, or sinful acts.

Besides "works of the flesh," the New Testament quite commonly uses a related term to describe sinful behavior; it speaks of "works of darkness" (Ephesians 5:11). In Bible lands, daytime and light are synonymous with heat; nighttime and darkness are identified with cold. In 1980 I presented a series of workers' meetings in Egypt. Afterward, the pastors took me to Mt. Sinai, where Moses received the Ten Commandments. During the day, the heat was terrible! It sometimes reached 112 degrees Fahrenheit. On the other hand, the nights were freezing cold, and I had neglected to take any warm clothing because we had left in the daytime when it was so hot! I had to borrow every piece of clothing I could in order to keep warm. Even in my sleeping bag, I was cold! I believe that is why God was a cloud to the Jews by day during the Exodus and a pillar of fire at night. By God's grace, He kept the Israelites warm at night and protected them from heat in the daytime. Apart from God's grace, the nights would have been unbearably cold. So works of darkness are the same as cold works. And both refer to sin, to works of the flesh.

What, then, are "hot works"? They must be the opposite of "cold works." If cold works represent works of the flesh, what would be the opposite? Would it not be "works of faith"?

In Galatians, chapter 5, Paul is contrasting the works of the flesh with the fruits of the Spirit. He says, "Walk in the Spirit, and ye shall not fulfil the lust of the flesh. For the flesh lusteth against the Spirit, and the Spirit against the flesh: and these are contrary the one to the other" (verses 16, 17). So the fruits of the Spirit are in opposition to the works of the flesh. And the fruits of the Spirit are the same as "works of faith." Jesus Himself makes this connection.

For example, Jesus said, "He that believeth on me [i.e., has faith in me], the works that I do shall he do also; and greater works than these shall he do; because I go unto my Father" (John 14:12). Now why would Jesus' followers be able to do even greater works because He

Laodicea is evaluated—I

was returning to His Father? Jesus answered this question in one of His last recorded conversations with His disciples before His death. "If I go not away, the Comforter will not come unto you; but if I depart, I will send him unto you" (John 16:7). In other words, "If I don't go to My Father, I will not be able to send you the Holy Spirit."

When we walk by faith, the Holy Spirit who lives in us will produce in our lives the works of Christ—works of faith. Works of faith always have their origin in the Holy Spirit. Faith says, "I am making myself available to you, Lord Jesus, because there is nothing good in me." Works of faith are the result of Christ living in us by faith. Paul says, "I am crucified with Christ: nevertheless I live; yet not I, but Christ liveth in me: and the life which I now live in the flesh I live by the faith of the Son of God who loved me, and gave himself for me" (Galatians 2:20).

How does Christ live in me? Through the Holy Spirit. Paul says:

> Ye are not in the flesh, but in the Spirit, if so be that the Spirit of God dwell in you. Now if any man have not the Spirit of Christ, he is none of his. And if Christ be in you, the body is dead because of sin; but the Spirit is life because of righteousness (Romans 8:9, 10).

In works of faith, the Spirit is actually the One doing the works; I am simply bearing fruit. When I look at works of faith from my perspective, they are not works; they are simply the fruit of the Holy Spirit, who is living in me.

Paul commends the believers at Thessalonica for their "work of faith" (1 Thessalonians 1:3). He urges Titus to affirm in his churches that those who have faith in God should maintain good works (see Titus 3:8). And James deals with works of faith as evidence of justification. "Was not Abraham our father justified by works, when he had offered Isaac his son upon the altar? Seest thou how faith wrought with his works, and by works was faith made perfect?" (James 2:21, 22).

LAODICEA

"Works of faith" and "the fruits of the Spirit" are, therefore, synonymous. These are the "hot works" Christ refers to in His letter to Laodicea.

We have seen, then, from the Scriptures that "cold works" represent "works of the flesh." "Hot works" represent "works of faith." What do "lukewarm works" represent? Lukewarm works represent a mixture of hot and cold works—an attempt to mingle works of the flesh with works of faith. The Bible describes these as "works of the law."

What does the Bible have to say about works of the law? A good starting point is Galatians 2:16, where Paul uses the phrase three times:

> Knowing that a man is not justified by the works of the law, but by the faith of Jesus Christ, even we have believed in Jesus Christ, that we might be justified by the faith of Christ, and not by the works of the law: for by the works of the law shall no flesh be justified.

In the next chapter, Paul gives the reason why works of the law cannot justify us. "As many as are of the works of the law are under the curse: for it is written, Cursed is every one that continueth not in all things which are written in the book of the law to do them" (Galatians 3:10).

What, exactly, does Paul mean by this phrase "works of the law"? He defines it for us in Philippians 3:9. He says that he wants to be "in him [Jesus Christ], not having mine own righteousness, which is of the law, but that which is through the faith of Christ." Righteousness that comes by works of the law is *self-righteousness*—a righteousness that is produced by self. Works of the law represent a self-righteousness produced through one's own efforts. We have a word for that in English; we call it *legalism*. The Greek language in New Testament times did not have a single word that was equivalent to what we mean in English by the term *legalism*. So Paul used the expression "works of the law" to express the same idea. Whenever you come across the phrase "works of the law" in Paul's writings, you can substitute the word *legalism*, and you will have the right idea. It refers to our efforts to keep the law as a means or method of salvation.

We have said that the cold works Jesus speaks about in His letter to Laodicea represent works of the flesh, or sin. We said that hot works represent works of faith, the fruit that is produced in our lives by the power of the Holy Spirit. Jesus, however, says that He knows Laodicea's works and that they are neither hot nor cold, but lukewarm. I believe that these lukewarm works represent works of the law—a legalistic self-righteousness that attempts to obey the law as a means of salvation. Let's see why this is so.

When a person goes about to establish his or her own righteousness through obedience to the law, who is doing the works—the Spirit or the flesh? Obviously, it is not the Holy Spirit at work. It is the individual self. So the flesh is the source of the works that are being done. However, the works themselves resemble the same works the Holy Spirit produces by faith in the life of the Christian. Outwardly, it may well be hard to tell the difference. For example, two individuals may both be visiting the sick. One is doing so as a result of the Spirit working in his life by faith. The other is doing so as a result of his own attempt to obey the law and thereby deserve salvation. The visible actions may look the same, but the source and motivation of the action are quite different. In other words, the flesh that belongs to sin (cold works) is doing outwardly the things that actually belong to the Spirit and faith (hot works). In this sense, works of the law are lukewarm works—a legalistic mixture of cold and hot, of the flesh imitating the Spirit.

You remember the young man who came to Jesus asking, "What good thing shall I do, that I may have eternal life?" (Matthew 19:16).

Jesus replied, "If you want to go to heaven by doing something good, you must keep the law."

LAODICEA

And the young man asked, "Which law? What specifically do You mean?"

"The six commandments that refer to our relationship with each other," Jesus answered.

What did the young man say next? "I've kept all these things since I was in the primary division of Sabbath School" (see verses 17-20).

The works this young man had been doing all his life were works of the law. "Works of the law" is the flesh trying to be good. So the works themselves look a lot like works of faith. For example: Does a person whose life is filled with works of faith keep the Sabbath? Certainly, he does. Does the person whose life is filled with works of the law keep the Sabbath? Of course. What is the difference? The difference may not be apparent outwardly. When we find a person keeping the Sabbath, the question is not: "Are you keeping the right day?" The question is: "Are you keeping the Sabbath based on works of faith or on works of law?" That's the important question.

So the difference between works of faith (hot works) and works of law (lukewarm works) is the motivation behind them, the reason for doing what we do. The acts themselves may be quite similar outwardly.

On the other hand, works of the law and works of the flesh are altogether different; the contrast between them is quite clear. Both originate from the flesh, but they are extreme opposites. The works of the flesh ("cold works") are sinful acts—adultery, hatred, lying, etc. The works of the law ("lukewarm works") are righteous acts—on the surface. That is why they are lukewarm—because the flesh is pretending to do the work of the Spirit. The cold is mixing itself with the hot. Works of law look good on the outside and therefore are very deceiving. It is very difficult to convince a self-righteous person that his outwardly good acts are all wrong.

Ellen White identifies Laodicea's problem in these same terms and agrees with the idea that lukewarmness is self-righteousness. She says, "Your self-righteousness is nauseating to the Lord Jesus Christ. . . .

Laodicea is evaluated—I

These words [Revelation 3:15-18] apply to the churches and to many of those in positions of trust in the work of God" (*The Seventh-day Adventist Bible Commentary*, 7:963).

So what is Laodicea's main problem? Self-righteousness. Jesus told a parable about a king who invited a great number of guests to his son's wedding feast. He provided special garments for each guest to wear to the banquet. But one man refused to wear the garment and attended in his own clothes. He was clothed in his own self-righteousness. "My suit is clean," he told the king. "I don't need your garment." Ellen White comments on this parable, "Self-righteousness is not the wedding garment. A failure to follow the clear light of truth is our fearful danger. The message to the Laodicean church reveals our condition as a people" (*Review and Herald*, 15 December 1904).

She also gives this insight into Christ's opinion of our self-righteousness:

> There are those who profess to serve God, while they rely upon their own efforts to obey His law, to form a right character, and secure salvation. Their hearts are not moved by any deep sense of the love of Christ, but they seek to perform the duties of the Christian life as that which God requires of them in order to gain heaven. Such a religion is worth nothing (*Steps to Christ*, 44).

Lukewarmness, a legalistic self-righteousness, is altogether worthless in the eyes of Jesus. In fact, in His message to Laodicea, the Faithful Witness makes a shocking statement. "I would rather you were cold than lukewarm," He says (see Revelation 3:15).

Does this mean that Jesus would prefer we actually go out and do sinful things, works of the flesh, rather than be lukewarm and try to do good things for the wrong reasons? Apparently so. Why would He say such a thing?

LAODICEA

Once, Jesus told the self-righteous Pharisees that it would fare better with Nineveh in the judgment than it would with Israel (see Matthew 12:41). When Jonah preached to the people of Nineveh that unless they repented they would be destroyed because of their wickedness (works of the flesh), they responded positively and repented before God. Nineveh's problem was open sin—the wicked works of the flesh—and they knew it. It wasn't difficult for God to convince them of their sinful condition.

But when God told the Israelites that their works of the law were all wrong, they felt insulted and rejected Him. They were blind to their condition because the works they were doing looked so good on the outside. These works came from the flesh, but they looked so good! We will find that Laodicea has the very same problem. Laodicea is blind to her true condition because her lukewarm works look so good on the outside.

One of the hardest things for us to do is to recognize our true condition. As long as we don't understand what we are really like, then the Faithful and True Witness's counsel is meaningless to us. Once we recognize our condition, we are well on our way to the solution.

You see, a doctor must first find out what is wrong with the patient before he can give him the correct medicine. My mother nearly died in Africa because a doctor gave her the wrong medicine. He was guessing at what was wrong with her; he wasn't sure. Does the True Witness know what is wrong with us? The answer is obvious. Can He heal us? Most certainly; He is the Great Physician. But before a doctor can perform an operation on you, he or she must obtain a signed surgical permission—at least in America. Likewise, before Jesus can cure us, He must get our permission to take out our hearts of stone and replace them with hearts of flesh. The moment we give Him permission, the cure is available. But we must first recognize our need; we must admit that His evaluation of our condition is accurate. We must admit that our problem is self-righteousness, which looks so good on

Laodicea is evaluated—I

the outside but is so nauseating to Christ.

But *why* does God object so to self-righteousness? Although it has its shortcomings, isn't self-righteousness better than no righteousness at all? Isn't it better to be lukewarm than to be cold? If your child is trying his best to please you, does that make you angry or happy? Naturally, it makes you happy. Yet here is a church that is trying its best to please God, and God is sick about it! Why? The answer is crucial. Why does Jesus say He would prefer Laodicea was cold than lukewarm?

We will turn to that question in the next chapter.

CHAPTER 3

LAODICEA
is evaluated—II

I know thy works, that thou art neither cold nor hot: I would thou wert cold or hot. So then because thou art lukewarm, and neither cold nor hot, I will spue thee out of my mouth.
REVELATION 3:15, 16

Have you ever bitten down on some grapes, thinking they were seedless, and they were not? What did you do? You spit out the seeds and the little pieces of seeds that had gotten chewed up, didn't you? And you felt a kind of relief when you had gotten rid of those seeds that you weren't expecting.

In the days of the New Testament, people hadn't yet learned how to produce seedless grapes or oranges. So when they came to seeds, they were expecting them. But they spit them out just the same. Consequently, the phrase "to spit out" or "to spew out" something became a way of saying you rejected that thing. To spit out something meant to reject it. That is the meaning of what Jesus says to Laodicea.

To those who are indifferent at this time, Christ's warning is: "Because thou art lukewarm, and neither cold nor hot, I will spew

LAODICEA

thee out of my mouth." Revelation 3:16. The figure of spewing out of His mouth means that He cannot offer up your prayers or your expressions of love to God. He cannot endorse your teaching of His Word or your spiritual work in anywise. He cannot present your religious exercises with the request that grace be given you (*Testimonies for the Church*, 6:408).

Here is the problem: Jesus says our works are neither hot nor cold, but lukewarm. He says He wishes we were either hot or cold. In other words, if we were hot, He would be happy. If we were cold, He would be able to correct that. But lukewarmness, He cannot abide. This is because both hot works and cold works are natural, but lukewarm works are not. What do I mean?

The flesh is sinful, so the natural thing for the flesh to produce is—what? Sin! When you and I commit sin, we are simply acting according to our natures, which are sinful.

Likewise, when the Spirit lives in us, it is natural for the Spirit to do righteousness. John says, "Whosoever is born of God doth not commit sin" (1 John 3:9). The new life that begins when the Holy Spirit lives in us does not sin, because the Spirit naturally does righteousness. So hot works are the natural result of the Holy Spirit, who lives in us. And cold works are the natural result of the flesh. But lukewarm works are not natural either to the flesh or to the Spirit. Therefore, when the flesh, which is sinful, pretends to be good through self-righteousness, such works are hypocritical and unnatural.

Before we consider why Christ rejects lukewarm works so strongly, let's look in more detail at exactly what lukewarm works really are. And in order to do that, let's see first what lukewarm works are *not*.

When Jesus tells us that our works are lukewarm, He is not saying that sometimes our works are hot and sometimes they are cold, so on average they are lukewarm. Some Bible students believe that this is the substance of Jesus' accusation against Laodicea. They believe He adds up the total picture of her works—some hot and some cold—and the average is only a lukewarm condition.

That is not at all what Jesus is saying. He is saying, "All the time, all your works are lukewarm." It's not that some are hot and some are cold; everything Laodicea is doing is lukewarm. We need to keep this important point in mind.

Second, some Adventists understand Laodicea's lukewarmness as a particular point in a process of moving from being hot to being cold. In the early days, they say, our church used to be hot. Our pioneers worked hard and sacrificed themselves and their possessions. But as we became a larger, more popular church, we became lukewarm. Once, we were hot, but we are moving toward being cold. Right now, we are sort of in-between; we have cooled off until we are only lukewarm and need revival. Those who understand Laodicea's lukewarmness in this way use Revelation 2:4, 5 to support the idea. "I have somewhat against thee, because thou hast left thy first love. Remember therefore from whence thou art fallen, and repent." The problem with using Revelation 2:4, 5 is that these verses are from Christ's message to the church at *Ephesus*, not Laodicea! Christ doesn't say to the Laodicean church, "You were once hot, but now have become lukewarm. Be careful, or I will spit you out!" No, Christ says to Laodicea, "You are neither hot nor cold, but lukewarm." Lukewarmness is Laodicea's chronic condition.

We can't apply Christ's message to Ephesus to our condition as Laodicea. It's true that the pioneers of this movement worked hard and sacrificed themselves. But what about the works they were doing—were they works of faith (hot works) or works of law (lukewarm works)? The evidence from Seventh-day Adventist history suggests that, like us, some of the early leaders of this church became trapped in a subtle form of legalism—that is, of lukewarm works.

In 1874 Uriah Smith, editor of *The Review and Herald* (we call it the *Adventist Review* today), published a four-month series of articles titled

LAODICEA

"Leading Doctrines of the Review." The articles had much to say about the law but *nothing* about justification by faith, which is the foundation of hot works.

Three years later, James White and Uriah Smith held a "Bible Institute" in Battle Creek, Michigan. This was a series of lectures for Adventist ministers, focusing on the Bible. The purpose was to train these pastors to go out and preach the three angels' messages more effectively. These lectures were later published, and once more, there was no mention made of justification by faith. The following year, 1878, Uriah Smith published a 336-page book, *Synopsis of Present Truth*. Again, this summary of the Adventist message contained no mention of justification by faith or of righteousness by faith. You can see why Christians of other faiths began to accuse Adventists of being legalists as they noted our focus on law and our neglect of righteousness by faith. It was in this context that Ellen White wrote, "We have preached the law until we are as dry as the hills of Gilboah that had neither dew nor rain. We must preach Christ in the law, and there will be sap and nourishment in the preaching" (*The Review and Herald*, 11 March 1890).

So when Jesus accuses us of being lukewarm, this is what He is talking about—works of the law, legalism, attempting to obey the law in our own strength in order to be saved, doing good things for the wrong reasons. And He warns us, "Because thou art lukewarm, and neither cold nor hot, I will spue thee out of my mouth" (Revelation 3:16)! This lukewarmness will cause Christ to reject us!

Why? Are lukewarm works bad works? Are they the same as works of the flesh (sin)? Not outwardly. Why, then, is God so opposed to lukewarm works? Here are four reasons self-righteousness, works of the law, are so nauseating to Christ that He will have to spit us out if we remain lukewarm.

1. Hypocrisy. In the previous chapter, we saw that our flesh, that is, our fallen human natures, are 100 percent sinful (see Romans 7:18). Therefore, when we try in the flesh to be good, when in our own strength we try to imitate God and His righteousness, that is "hypocrisy." Paul calls it "a fair shew in the flesh" (Galatians 6:12). In the Galatian church, the issue was circumcision; for us, the issue could be Sabbath keeping, dress, diet, or any one of many things. But the principle is the same: The flesh is trying to be good and to show others how good it can be.

Matthew 23 is dealing with what Jesus thinks of self-righteousness, works of the law. In this chapter, He is evaluating the Pharisees, who were experts at works of the law. He told the people, "The scribes and the Pharisees sit in Moses' seat: All therefore whatsoever they bid you observe, that observe and do; but do not ye after their works" (verses 2, 3). In other words, Jesus recognized the scribes and Pharisees as the authorities in interpreting Moses' law; they were the experts. The Pharisees were extremely zealous regarding the law of Moses.

Jesus did not argue with the religious leaders regarding the law. They were teaching good things. He even told the people to observe what their leaders told them to do (see verse 3). But He warned the people not to do as their leaders did. Why? The problem was not with the Pharisees' understanding of the law, but with the motive behind their works. "All their works," Jesus said, "they do for to be seen of men" (verse 5). What they were doing was good, but *why* were they doing it? They were doing it as a way of saying "See how good I am!" They wanted everyone to see. Jesus called them "hypocrites" and "blind guides" (verses 13-16). "Woe unto you, scribes and Pharisees, hypocrites! for ye are like unto whited sepulchres, which indeed appear beautiful outward, but are within full of dead men's bones, and of all uncleanness. Even so ye also outwardly appear righteous unto men, but within ye are full of hypocrisy and iniquity" (verses 27, 28).

This attitude of the Pharisees and scribes may also be our attitude as well. Ellen White tells us:

> We may have flattered ourselves, as did Nicodemus [Nicodemus

LAODICEA

was a member of the Sanhedrin, so he was a first-class Pharisee], that our life has been upright, that our moral character is correct, and think that we need not humble the heart before God, like the common sinner: but when the light from Christ shines into our souls, we shall see how impure we are; we shall discern the selfishness of motive, the enmity against God, that has defiled every act of life (*Steps to Christ*, 28, 29).

We all face this problem of self-righteousness in different forms. At times when I stand at the entrance to the church after a Sabbath sermon, someone will say to me, "That was an excellent sermon." And to myself, my flesh will reply, "You worked hard to produce that sermon, didn't you? It really was a very good sermon!" Then I have to say to myself, "Get thee behind me, Satan!" (I don't say that out loud, of course, because the church member might think I was insulting him!) Satan will encourage the flesh to raise its ugly head whenever possible. Notice Ellen White is dealing in this statement with *motive*, not with the outward action itself. She says, "We shall discern the selfishness of motive."

We need to ask ourselves, "Why am I doing the things that I do?" For example, do I go out and work hard giving Bible studies because I want to share God's truth with others? Or because I want to impress the church? Or because I want to impress God? Or because I think it will help ensure my salvation? Am I performing works of faith or works of the law? That's the question. What is the source of the works that I do—the Spirit or the flesh?

Obviously, we cannot determine another person's motive for what he or she does. That is why we must never judge each other. We have enough difficulty understanding our own motives. One way to discover if your own motives are selfish is to ask yourself: "When I'm successful in God's work, do I have a tendency to look down on those who are having failure?" Be warned; this is the flesh trying to tell you

Laodicea is evaluated—II

how good you are! The flesh doesn't want to give the Holy Spirit the glory, because the flesh is the enemy of the Spirit.

The first reason, then, that God rejects self-righteousness, or works of the law, is because the motive is all wrong. We may be doing the right things, but for the wrong reasons. The Jews in Jesus' day were keeping the Sabbath. In fact, they were very strict and had all sorts of rules to make sure they didn't desecrate God's holy day. But they kept the Sabbath from selfish motives—so that they might be saved and so that God would bless them.

2. *Unbelief.* The second reason self-righteousness is so nauseating to Christ is that in reality it is based on unbelief. Jesus says, "Without me ye can do nothing" (John 15:5).

If you say, "No, God, You're wrong; I *can* do something good," then are you exhibiting belief in Him or unbelief? Clearly, you are exhibiting unbelief. Let me give you some examples.

When, shortly before His crucifixion, Jesus said to the disciples, "All of you will forsake Me this night" (see Matthew 26:30-35), did they agree? No. What were they guilty of? Unbelief.

When God showed Peter that the gospel was not only for Jews but for Gentiles also, did Peter agree? No. God had to tell him, "What I have cleansed, don't ever call unclean" (see Acts 9-16). God was correcting Peter's unbelief.

Any time we deny God's verdict on the flesh, we are exhibiting unbelief. That is exactly what is happening in Laodicea's reaction to Christ's message. The True Witness says that we are "wretched, and miserable, and poor, and blind, and naked." What is Laodicea's response? "I am rich, and increased with goods, and have need of nothing" (Revelation 3:17). Who is right? Is Jesus telling the truth about us, or do you believe that He is making a mistake? We may admit with the lips that Jesus is correct, but our temptation is to point to our glowing reports of the works that we do and say, "But our works are so good."

LAODICEA

What did Jesus mean when He told Nicodemus, "That which is born of the flesh is flesh" (John 3:6)? Was He not saying, "Let me tell you the facts, Nicodemus. Your flesh, your sinful human nature, can never produce righteousness. You can produce righteousness only if you are born from above of the Spirit."

No matter how good our works of the law may appear in our sight, we must remember that they are always based on unbelief. Whenever the flesh tries to do something that God has said it cannot do, we are saying, in effect, "God, You are a liar." And that is unbelief. That is why works of the law are always based on unbelief.

3. *Selfishness.* Paul says, Love *(agape)* "seeketh not her own" (1 Corinthians 13:5). There is no selfishness in *agape*. Therefore, if we do anything from a selfish motive, we are in opposition to the principle of *agape* love—the true motivation for all works of faith. Peter came to Jesus once and said, "We have forsaken all, and followed thee; what shall we have therefore?" (Matthew 19:27). Why did Peter forsake all? Was that a work of the law or a work of faith? His motive was selfish; he believed that Jesus would overthrow the Romans, and he wanted to be one of the top cabinet ministers in the new government. He forsook everything to follow Jesus, but his motive was a selfish one, and thus his sacrifice was a work of the law.

How can we be sure? Because when Jesus came to wash Peter's feet in the upper room, Peter said, "You will never wash my feet."

Now, Jesus knew Peter's heart, so He said, "If I don't wash your feet, you will have no part in My kingdom." To Peter, this meant, "Forget your prime ministers position!"

"Oh," Peter said, in effect, "in that case, wash not only my feet, but my head and my hands, because I want to be prime minister."

Works of the law may appear good on the outside, but they are devoid of *agape*. They are based on selfish motives, and therefore they are as filthy rags to God (see Isaiah 64:6). "Love to God is the very foundation of religion. To engage in His service merely from hope of

Laodicea is evaluated—II

reward or fear of punishment would avail nothing" (*Patriarchs and Prophets*, 523).

4. *Denying Christ.* The final reason that Christ is nauseated by works of the law is because they deny Christ as our righteousness. Paul emphatically told the Galatians, "Christ is become of no effect unto you, whosoever of you are justified by the law" (Galatians 5:4). What was the problem in the Galatian church? Was it the same problem the Jews were having? No. The Jews wanted salvation entirely by their own works. The Galatian Christians fell for another of Satan's traps. It was legalism, to be sure, but it was a subtle form of legalism. The Galatians fell for the idea that it isn't enough to accept Christ as our righteousness. We must also contribute to His righteousness by keeping the law—in their case, by being circumcised. In other words, the Galatian problem was the idea: "I am saved by faith *plus* works."

Ellen White speaks to this issue specifically. "Should faith plus works purchase the gift of salvation for anyone, then the Creator is under obligation to the creature. Here is an opportunity for falsehood to be accepted as truth" (*Faith and Works*, 20). This is where the Roman Catholic Church has gone wrong. The Catholic Church teaches that a person is saved by faith plus penance. When I was a Roman Catholic and went to confession, I did not come out of the confessional box free from my sins. I had to do penance following my confession. Now, we teenagers were smart! We would watch to see which priest was hearing confessions in which box, because some priests gave us long penances to perform, and others gave short penances. We always waited in the long line for a kindhearted priest. Those in the short lines were mainly older people who wanted to do long penances because they felt that the more penance they did, the more God would accept them. All we teenagers wanted was to get our penance over with as quickly as possible. Ellen White says that if we add works to our faith, we are no different from the Catholics who add penance to confession.

Both imputed righteousness (justification) and imparted righteous-

LAODICEA

ness (sanctification) must be all of Christ. The world needs to see not us, but Christ living in us and through us. Only when Christ lives in us through the Holy Spirit will we do the works of Christ from the motive of pure *agape* love. Then the world will be lightened with God's glory (see Revelation 18). And that is Christ's real objective in giving the Laodicean message. May it be realized soon!

CHAPTER 4

LAODICEA
is deceived

Thou sayest, I am rich, and increased with goods, and have need of nothing; and knowest not that thou art wretched, and miserable, and poor, and blind, and naked.
REVELATION 3:17

In His message to Laodicea, the True Witness shows us clearly that our lukewarmness—our self-righteousness, or legalism—has deceived us. Revelation 3:17 divides naturally into two parts. The first half of the verse is Laodicea's own opinion of her spiritual condition; the second half is Christ's evaluation of Laodicea's condition. And it is clear that the two opinions disagree totally. There is a radical contradiction between what we think of ourselves and what Christ sees in us.

Laodicea's problem is a subconscious one. Jesus says Laodicea "knowest not" that she is wretched and miserable and blind and naked. In other words, we have been deceived regarding our true spiritual condition. We do not know what we are really like.

What greater deception can come upon human minds than a

LAODICEA

confidence that they are right when they are all wrong! The message of the True Witness finds the people of God in a sad deception, yet honest in that deception. They know not that their condition is deplorable in the sight of God. While those addressed are flattering themselves that they are in an exalted spiritual condition, the message of the True Witness breaks their security by the startling denunciation of their true condition of spiritual blindness, poverty, and wretchedness. The testimony so cutting and severe, cannot be a mistake, for it is the True Witness who speaks, and His testimony must be correct (*Testimonies for the Church*, 3:252, 253).

Now, it is easy to tell the difference between hot works and cold ones—between works of faith and works of the flesh. That is not why Laodicea is deceived about her condition. The reason we have been deceived is that we have not clearly distinguished works *of the law* (lukewarm works) from works of faith (hot works). It is easy to confuse these two, for the difference between works of the law and works of faith is a real, but subtle, difference.

Luther himself confused these two kinds of works when he condemned the apostle James for upholding works of faith. He called James's epistle "an epistle of straw" because he felt that James contradicted Paul's writings in the New Testament and that Paul was correct. Actually, Paul and James agree completely. Both uphold works of faith; both teach that genuine justification by faith always produces works of faith. (Later in his life, Luther reversed his opinion of James, admitting that the apostle was correct and inspired.)

Paul condemns works of the law—self-righteousness—but he insists on works of faith. "By the deeds [or works] of the law there shall no flesh be justified in his sight" (Romans 3:20). Paul condemns any effort to get to heaven by performing works of the law; those who try to be righteous by keeping the law will never succeed. "Therefore,"

Laodicea is deceived

Paul says, "we conclude that a man is justified by faith without the deeds of the law" (verse 28). He taught the same thing to the Galatian Christians. "A man is not justified by the works of the law, but by the faith of Jesus Christ, even we have believed in Jesus Christ, that we might be justified by the faith of Christ, and not by the works of the law: for by the works of the law shall no flesh be justified" (Galatians 2:16). In other words, works of the law contradict justification by faith; they are enemies of the gospel. "Satan is seeking with all his subtlety to corrupt mind and heart. And oh how successful he is in leading men and women to depart from the simplicity of the gospel of Christ. . . . Church members are in danger of allowing self to take the throne" (*Review and Herald*, 15 December 1904).

Works of the law are what we call legalism or self-righteousness. Such works have no part in our justification. We are justified solely by what Christ did for us in His life and death. Paul explicitly condemns anyone who tries to add works of the law to justification by faith. "Christ is become of no effect unto you, whosoever of you are justified by the law; ye are fallen from grace" (Galatians 5:4). Justification by faith simply cannot mix with works of the law; they are mutually exclusive.

On the other hand, Paul strenuously upholds works of faith! After insisting that works do not contribute one bit to our salvation (see Ephesians 2:8, 9), Paul tells the believers that nevertheless, "we are . . . created in Christ Jesus unto good works, which God hath before ordained that we should walk in them" (verse 10). Thus Paul is in harmony with James, who is arguing that justification by faith always produces works of faith.

To the young pastor, Titus, Paul writes, "Not by works of righteousness which we have done [that is, works of the law], but according to his [God's] mercy he saved us" (Titus 3:5). Yet only three verses later, Paul says, "I will that thou affirm constantly, that they which have believed in God might be careful to maintain good works. These things are good and profitable unto men" (verse 8). Notice that works

LAODICEA

of faith are profitable, not to us, but "unto men." Good works reveal to others what Christ is doing in us. It testifies that genuine justification by faith is present.

In this same letter to Titus, Paul says that Christ "gave himself for us, that he might redeem us from all iniquity, and purify unto himself a peculiar people, zealous of good works" (Titus 2:14). The Greek word translated "zealous" comes from the same root as the word translated "hot" in Revelation 3:15. Paul clearly supports good works—not as a way to earn our salvation, but as a means of demonstrating genuine justification by faith and of drawing others to Christ. Thus Paul and James are in complete harmony.

"But," some will argue, "didn't the heroes of the Old Testament win God's favor by their works—by keeping His laws?"

Not at all. Hebrews, chapter 11 explicitly commends numerous Old Testament individuals for their good works and obedience, but they are commended because of their works of *faith*. The phrase "by faith" is repeated over and over in Hebrews 11. For example, "By faith Abraham, when he was called to go out into a place which he should after receive for an inheritance, obeyed; and he went out, not knowing whither he went" (verse 8).

Abraham didn't know where he was going, but he obeyed God's call. It was an obedience born of faith. He didn't ask God (as some missionaries ask the General Conference), "Is there electricity where I'm going? Are there refrigerators?" God didn't tell Abraham, "There is a house waiting there for you with running water." He simply said, "I want you to go to a land that I will give you." And Abraham obeyed *in faith*; therefore, his actions were works of faith, not works of the law, even though he certainly obeyed God's commandments.

Likewise with Noah. God said to Noah, "I'm going to destroy this earth with a flood. I want you to build an ark." Did Noah believe God? Yes, and his works gave evidence of his faith. True works of faith are always built on the promises of *God*; works of the law are built on

Laodicea is deceived

human promises and performance. At Sinai, God said to the Israelites, "Here are My laws."

And they replied, "All that You say, *we* will do" (see Exodus 24:7).

What, then, is the essential difference between works of the law and works of faith? Why have we become so deceived that we have mistaken the one for the other and have become unconscious of our real spiritual condition? If we are going to be able to respond to Christ's counsel, we need to have our eyes open so that we can see clearly the essential difference that sets works of the law apart from works of faith.

The difference is not in the works themselves, because works of the law and works of faith appear very similar outwardly. There can be two people keeping the Sabbath. One is doing so as a work of law; the other as a work of faith. There can be two people giving Bible studies. One is doing so as a work of law; the other as a work of faith. The actions look similar on the outside; what is the difference?

The first difference is in *the source or origin* of the work that is being done. Works of the law are done through human effort—by the flesh. Works of faith are done by Christ through His Spirit because the Christian is walking by faith. Let's look at an example of each.

An excellent example of works of the law is the Pharisee's prayer in Luke 18. The introduction to this story is crucial. Notice that Jesus told this story in the context of self-righteousness, or works of the law. "He spake this parable unto certain [people] *who trusted in themselves that they were righteous, and despised others*" (Luke 18:9, emphasis supplied). Works of the law typically cause us to despise others; legalists tend to look down on those who aren't measuring up to their standards.

> Two men went up into the temple to pray; the one a Pharisee, and the other a publican. The Pharisee stood and prayed thus with himself, God, I thank thee, that I am not as other men are, extortioners, unjust, adulterers, or even as this publican. I fast

LAODICEA

twice in the week, I give tithes of all that I possess (verses 10-12).

Now, to Jesus' listeners, the word *Pharisee* didn't have the negative meaning it has to us today. A Pharisee was considered to be a very holy person because he was zealous to keep God's law. So this is a good person who is telling God about himself. Are his works good or bad? They are good! He would get a star in his crown if we were passing them out! But were these good things that he did works of the law or works of faith?

They were works of the law. Why? What is wrong with this Pharisee's works?

They made him feel good about himself. He wasn't living for God, but for himself. He's telling God, "Please look at me. See how good I am!"

And what will Jesus say to him in the judgment? "Many will say to me in that day, Lord, Lord, have we not prophesied in thy name? and in thy name have cast out devils? and in thy name done many wonderful works? And then I will profess unto them, I never knew you: depart from me, ye that work iniquity" (Matthew 7:22, 23). "The people of God are represented in the message to the Laodiceans as in a position of carnal security. They are at ease, believing themselves to be in an exalted condition of spiritual attainments" (*Testimonies for the Church*, 3:252).

Works of the law are always done for ourselves, for *our* glory. The source is the flesh, our sinful human nature. The flesh cannot do genuine good works. It can perform works that appear good, but the source is wrong because the flesh is always dominated by self. Notice how often the Pharisee in Jesus' story uses the word *I* as he prays about himself.

In contrast, let's consider this example of works of faith. Paul, who was also a Pharisee, discarded all his works of the law in exchange for Christ and His righteousness.

Laodicea is deceived

For we [genuine Christians] . . . worship God in the spirit, and rejoice in Christ Jesus, and have no confidence in the flesh. . . . [I want to be] found in him [Jesus], not having mine own righteousness, which is of the law, but that which is through the faith of Christ, the righteousness which is of God by faith: That I may know him, and the power of his resurrection, and the fellowship of his sufferings (Philippians 3:3, 9).

Paul's confidence was in Jesus Christ, not in himself. He says, "I want Jesus to live in me now that I've accepted Him as my righteousness." That must be our position also. Our confidence must be in Jesus, not in self.

Writing to the Corinthian church, Paul says, "I laboured more abundantly than they all [the other apostles]." But lest someone should misunderstand, he quickly adds, "Yet not I, but the grace of God which was with me" (1 Corinthians 15:10). It wasn't Paul, in his human nature, who was doing the work; it was God doing it in him. The source of works of faith is Christ working in us through His Spirit.

That is the first difference between works of the law and works of faith. Works of the law have their source in our sinful human natures. Works of faith have their origin in Jesus Christ, who works in us and through us by His Spirit.

The second difference between the two is closely related. It is the motive that lies behind the works that we do.

Works of the law are motivated by one or more of the following reasons: (1) fear of punishment; (2) desire for reward; (3) bringing glory to self. Works of the law are always motivated by self. They are self pretending to be good.

God judges us, not by our actions, but by the motives behind those actions. Our problem as Laodicea—the reason we are deceived about our true condition—is that we do the opposite; we judge ourselves by our actions, not by our motives. Jesus brought out this distinction in

LAODICEA

His Sermon on the Mount. The Pharisee would say, "I have never murdered anyone!" But Jesus replies, "Wait a minute! If you hate someone in your heart, you have killed him, even if you don't actually murder him physically. If you look at a woman with lust in your heart, you have committed adultery, even if you haven't actually done the act." God looks at the heart. That is why in the judgment He will weigh every secret motive. When we realize this far-reaching standard, we will know that all of us are unclean. "All the ways of a man are clean in his own eyes; but the Lord weigheth the spirits" (Proverbs 16:2). God considers not only the act, but the spirit that motivates the act.

Paul illustrates the difference between works of the law and works of faith by pointing to the experience of Abraham and his sons, Isaac and Ishmael. He says, "Abraham had two sons, the one by a bondmaid, the other by a freewoman. . . . He who was of the bondwoman was born after the flesh; but he of the freewoman was by promise" (Galatians 4:22, 23).

What does Paul mean? He is simply pointing out that Ishmael was the product of Abraham's own works. Isaac, on the other hand, was Abraham's son as the result of a promise. Who produced Ishmael? Abraham. Who produced Isaac? God. Abraham could not produce Isaac without a miracle from God because Sarah was past the age of childbearing. It was humanly impossible. Thus, works of faith are produced by God alone as we walk in faith as Abraham did. But works of the law are produced by our own human natures as Abraham produced Ishmael through Hagar. "Which things," Paul continues, "are an allegory: for these are the two covenants; the one from the mount Sinai, which gendereth to bondage" (verse 24).

Why is Mount Sinai a symbol of the covenant that leads to bondage? Because when God gave Israel His law on Mount Sinai, the people responded, "All that the Lord hath said we will do, and be obedient" (Exodus 24:7). That was the old covenant—people promising God to be good in exchange for salvation. Did they succeed? No. When they failed, did they acknowledge their failure? No. Instead, they made many rules—human rules—that they could keep. Then they said, "Look, God, we're keeping Your law."

The difference between the old covenant (Ishmael) and the new covenant (Isaac) is not easily apparent. Only a closer look at the two covenants reveals that while the old covenant was a *contract* between God and Israel, the new covenant was a *will* made by God, benefitting humanity. When God entered into a contract with Israel at Mount Sinai, He was fully aware they could not keep it. But the old covenant was necessary to destroy all confidence in the flesh so that the way might be opened for the new covenant. Unfortunately, the Jewish nation refused to acknowledge their total depravity and consequently rejected the new covenant in Christ. Their history, says Paul, has been recorded for our benefit "upon whom the ends of the world are come" (1 Corinthians 10:11). May we not repeat their history!

Paul continues his comparison, "But Jerusalem which is above is free, which is the mother of us all. . . . Now we, brethren, as Isaac was, are the children of promise" (Galatians 4:26, 28). Isaac represents God's promise and God's performance through Sarah. In the new covenant, we accept by faith the promises of God and allow Him to work in us. Here is how Ellen White puts it:

> There are those who profess to serve God, while they rely upon their own efforts to obey His law, to form a right character, and secure salvation. Their hearts are not moved by any deep sense of the love of Christ, but they seek to perform the duties of the Christian life as that which God requires of them in order to gain heaven. Such religion is worth nothing (*Steps to Christ*, 44).

The birth of a son to Zacharias, like the birth of the child of Abraham, and that of Mary [Christ Himself], was to teach a great spiritual truth, a truth that we are slow to learn and ready to for-

LAODICEA

get. In ourselves we are incapable of doing any good thing; but that which we cannot do will be wrought by the power of God in every submissive and believing soul. It was through faith that the child of promise was given. It is through faith that spiritual life is begotten, and we are enabled to do the works of righteousness (*The Desire of Ages*, 98).

It is only through faith that we can produce righteousness. Both justification and sanctification are by faith alone. "All our good works are dependent on a power outside of ourselves" (*Christ's Object Lessons*, 160). (Notice Ellen White says "*all* our good works," not "some of our good works.") "All that man can do without Christ is polluted with selfishness and sin; but that which is wrought through faith is acceptable to God" (*Selected Messages*, 1:364).

This is still an issue today with us in Laodicea. Many are trapped in a subtle form of legalism and are sincerely ignorant of it. Laodicea has been deceived, and she doesn't know it because she has confused works of the law with works of faith.

Some are concerned that if we teach these things, men and women will be tempted to quit trying to be obedient. That they will put forth no effort to overcome sin. But true faith always involves effort and struggle with sin. What does faith mean? It means two things when we truly put faith into practice. It means (1) "Not I," (2) "but Christ." The first is negative; this is our part. The second is positive; this is Christ's part.

The first is the most difficult. When we say, "Not I," we are saying something that contradicts our sinful human natures and our pride. We are going against our natures. Of course, that is painful to the ego because we want some credit in this matter of sanctification. So instead of saying, "Not I, but Christ," we prefer to say, "I *plus* Christ." We are willing to admit that justification is Christ alone, faith alone. But when it comes to sanctification, we want to have a part. But that is not true; the Bible does not teach that. The Bible teaches that the flesh, our human nature, is an enemy of God. It is not subject to God's law and never can be (see Romans 8:7). So in everything, we must say, "Not I, but Christ." That is what Christ is saying to poor, deceived Laodicea (see 2 Corinthians 4:7).

Our works, which look good because they are works of the law, have deceived us. They resemble works of faith, so we think that we are "rich, and increased with goods, and have need of nothing." But Christ says, Actually, you are "wretched, and miserable, and poor, and blind, and naked" (Revelation 3:17). The only other place in the New Testament where this word *wretched* appears is Romans 7:24. After admitting his inability in himself to do any good thing, Paul cries out, "O wretched man that I am! who shall deliver me from the body of this death?"

It's true that Paul also says, "I can do all things through Christ which strengtheneth me" (Philippians 4:13). But he can say that only after he has first said, "O wretched man that I am!" And the only way Paul or we can realize our wretchedness is to realize that our works of the law, good as they may appear, are as filthy rags in God's sight (see Isaiah 64:6).

When we do works of the law, the more we do, the more highly we think of ourselves—just like the Pharisee in Jesus' story. Those who are successfully doing works of the law are likely to believe, or even say, "I have not sinned for such and such a length of time." This is the epitome of the Laodicean condition! This attitude will destroy us!

In contrast, the believer who is doing works of faith will always see himself as a sinner. Even though his works are good, he will never feel righteous; he will always think of himself as "O wretched man that I am!" The closer we come to Christ, the more clearly we'll be able to see the great gulf between what we are and what He would have us to be. Ellen White says:

LAODICEA

The Laodicean message must be proclaimed with power; for now it is especially applicable. . . . Not to see our own deformity is not to see the beauty of Christ's character. When we are fully awake to our own sinfulness, we shall appreciate Christ. . . . Not to see the marked contrast between Christ and ourselves is not to know ourselves. He who does not abhor himself cannot understand the meaning of redemption (*Review and Herald*, 25 September 1900).

Of course, we may recognize that the righteousness of Christ dwells in us by faith. We may rejoice in the high esteem that Christ places on us "in Christ." But when we truly understand the gospel, sanctification—what Christ does in us—can never be the source of our assurance, because we will always feel that we are sinners—and that is no assurance! Our assurance comes from what we are "in Christ." In Christ, we stand complete and perfect. What He does in us is ongoing and imcomplete. In fact, Christ will do many good works in us that we are not even aware of. Remember, Jesus tells us that in the judgment He will say, "I was hungry, and you fed Me. I was thirsty, and you gave Me something to drink. I was naked, and you clothed Me."

And we will reply, "Lord, when did we do these things? We don't remember doing that." We are unconscious of many of the works Christ will do through us. Works of faith, what Christ does in us, do not save us. They are the *evidence* that we have salvation and justification by faith.

Laodicea is sadly deceived, mistaking her works of the law for works of faith. She looks at all the good things she is doing and says, "I am rich and need nothing!" But the True Witness sees that in reality, she is poor and blind and naked. May God give us grace to understand our true condition so that we will be willing to make a positive response to His counsel. And that is the topic of our next chapter.

CHAPTER 5

LAODICEA
is counseled

I counsel thee to buy of me gold tried in the fire, that thou mayest be rich; and white raiment, that thou mayest be clothed, and that the shame of thy nakedness do not appear; and anoint thine eyes with eyesalve, that thou mayest see
REVELATION 3:18

We need to thank God that the True Witness does not close His message to Laodicea with the evaluation of verse 17. After shattering our false security by telling us how wretched, miserable, poor, blind, and naked we truly are, Jesus goes on to reassure us that our situation is not hopeless. He offers a complete remedy for our problem. There is hope!

Just as Laodicea's problems are many, so Christ has a multiple solution. He says, I counsel you to buy from Me (1) "gold tried in the fire, that thou mayest be rich"; (2) "white raiment, that thou mayest be clothed"; and (3) "eyesalve, that thou mayest see" (verse 18).

As a solution to our poverty and wretchedness, Christ offers us gold purified in the fire so that we may be even richer than we think we are! For our miserable nakedness, He offers us white raiment so that we

LAODICEA

will not appear unclothed in the judgment. And for our blindness, He offers eye salve so that we may be able to see clearly our true condition. This is the threefold remedy Jesus offers for our threefold condition.

But note a very important phrase in His solution. "I counsel thee *to buy* of me . . ." The precious heavenly merchandise Christ offers us is not free. There is a price to be paid. Normally, these things and what they signify in Scripture are presented as free gifts of God. Then why does Jesus tell Laodicea that she must buy them?

They are free gifts only to those who are poor in spirit. But for the self-righteous, like Laodicea, they are not free; they come with a price. Israel had the same problem as Laodicea—self-righteousness. Through Isaiah, God gave His sales pitch to Israel. "Ho, every one that thirsteth, come ye to the waters, and he that hath no money; come ye, buy, and eat; yea, come, buy wine and milk without money and without price" (Isaiah 55:1). Now this makes no sense; in fact, it seems to be a contradiction. How can a person buy something if he has no money? And if he can buy without money, what is the price?

We need to understand how the word *buy* is being used here. It's being used the same way we use it in everyday speech—to exchange something you have for something you want more. In Bible times, people often exchanged goods in a barter system. If a person had too much corn growing in his garden, he would exchange it for wheat, perhaps. No money changed hands, but that was "buying" wheat, as far as the people in Bible times were concerned.

It really isn't any different if we use money as the medium of exchange. Let's say you pass a shop and see a lovely pair of shoes in the window. The price tag reads "$150." You say to yourself, "They are expensive, but I like them. Should I get them or not?" Now, you have $150 in your pocket. It's yours; you earned it through hard work. But the question you have to decide is: "Should I give up my money for this pair of shoes?" That is what buying is—exchanging something

Laodicea is counseled

you have for something you want more.

Laodicea may be poor in reality, but she does have something that is very valuable to her. It is her self-righteousness, produced by her works of the law. That is the basis of her pride—the basis of our pride, even our denominational pride. When a person, or a group of people, has had great success in the religious life, it isn't easy to give it up for the righteousness of Jesus Christ. The history of the Jews demonstrates this, as does the history of our own Seventh-day Adventist Church in 1888. The more outward success we have, the harder it is to discard it all for the righteousness of Jesus. It costs a great deal to do that; it's terribly expensive. Paul says:

> I might also have confidence in the flesh. If any other man thinketh that he hath whereof he might trust in the flesh, I more. Circumcised the eighth day, of the stock of Israel, of the tribe of Benjamin, an Hebrew of the Hebrews. . . . But what things were gain to me, those I counted loss for Christ. Yea doubtless, and I count all things but loss for the excellency of the knowledge of Christ Jesus my Lord: for whom I have suffered the loss of all things, and do count them but dung, that I may win Christ (Philippians 3:4, 5, 7, 8).

Paul was extremely successful as a Pharisee, yet he was willing to count all his successes as mere trash in comparison to the righteousness of Christ. When the True Witness says to Laodicea, "I counsel thee to buy of me gold tried in the fire," He is saying, "You must give up your self-righteousness, which you think has made you so rich, in exchange for My righteousness." That isn't easy to do, and the more self-righteousness we have, the more difficult it is to exchange it for the righteousness of Jesus. Ellen White says:

> The people of God are represented in the message to the

LAODICEA

Laodiceans as in a position of carnal [fleshly] security. They are at ease, believing themselves to be in an exalted condition of spiritual attainment (*Testimonies for the Church*, 3:252).

I asked the meaning of the shaking I had seen [in the church] and was shown that it would be caused by the straight testimony called forth by the counsel of the True Witness to the Laodiceans. This will have its effect upon the heart of the receiver, and will lead him to exalt the standard and pour forth the straight truth. Some will not bear this straight testimony. They will rise up against it, and this will cause a shaking among God's people (*Testimonies for the Church*, 1:181).

They [pastors] are not willing to be deprived of the garments of their own self-righteousness. They are not willing to exchange their own righteousness, which is unrighteousness, for the righteousness of Christ, which is pure unadulterated truth (*Testimonies to Ministers*, 65).

The flesh does not give up its own righteousness without a fight. It happened in this church in 1888, and it continues to happen. The flesh says, "I worked hard for this righteousness. Why should I give it up?" But there is no room for a mixture of self in the pure gospel of Christ our righteousness. Our attitude must continually be, "Not I, but Christ."

If anyone in the Jewish church was famous for self-righteousness, if there was anyone who could claim wonderful success, it was the apostle Paul before his conversion. He was without equal whether judged on the basis of his birth, his status as a Pharisee, or his law performance. It was his zeal for God that caused him to persecute the early Christians. Yet Paul was willing to give up all this success for the righteousness of Christ. He says, "Lord, I was on fire for You, and when I per-

Laodicea is counseled

secuted Christians, I wasn't doing it in rebellion against You. In my mind, I was serving You. Regarding the righteousness of the law, I was blameless. But those things that I thought were going to qualify me for heaven, I have come to count as rubbish compared to Christ and His righteousness" (see Philippians 3:4-9).

Paul was willing to give up all his religious success in exchange for Christ's righteousness. That is what the True Witness is talking about when He counsels Laodicea to "buy" gold, white clothing, and eye salve. We give up our self-righteousness, which means so much to us, in exchange for Christ's righteousness, which can alone make us rich and clothed and able to see.

But notice that this exchange involves suffering. Paul says, "I count all things but loss for the excellency of the knowledge of Christ Jesus my Lord: for whom I have suffered the loss of all things" (Philippians 3:8). It hurts our pride, individually and denominationally, when we give up all that we have attained through our hard work in order to accept Christ's righteousness. It's painful to our human natures. But we have only two options: we can cling to our own self-righteousness, which we have developed by much effort, or we can accept Christ's righteousness, which we receive by faith alone. We cannot have both; we must give up one or the other. That is the price we have to pay; it's a costly price, but it is the only solution to our Laodicean problems.

When the True Witness asks us to "buy" from Him gold and white clothing and eye salve, He is asking us to give up everything—our opinion about ourselves, all that we have thought was profit to us, but is not. All this we must exchange for Christ's righteousness, both in terms of our justification and our sanctification. The formula for both is the same—"Not I, but Christ." That's an expensive price, but it is what is required to "buy" the goods the True Witness offers. Are we willing to give up self and all the success that has given us "stars in our crown"? Are we willing to give up all for the righteousness of Christ? That is the price Paul the Pharisee had to pay, and it is the price we

LAODICEA

must pay as well.

That is why Ellen White says the counsel of the True Witness to Laodicea will produce a shaking in the church. Because some—especially those who have been successful in developing self-righteousness—will not be willing to pay this price. People who successfully produce self-righteousness usually have very strong wills. If you've held a "Breathe Free" stop-smoking program, you know that strong-willed persons have greater success than weak-willed persons. Strong-willed persons give the rest of us a hard time in committee meetings, and they often give sinners a hard time in discipline committees. They come down hard on people. They say, "Look, why is this person having such a problem with smoking? I used to be a heavy smoker, and I gave it up. It was nothing. Why can't this person do the same?"

Never forget that God views all our spiritual successes as filthy rags. Whatever we think is valuable in terms of our own spiritual achievements is, in God's eyes, tainted and impure. "We are all as an unclean thing, and all our righteousnesses are as filthy rags; and we all do fade as a leaf; and our iniquities [our self-righteousness], like the wind, have taken us away" (Isaiah 64:6).

We have examined the meaning of the word *buy* in the True Witness's counsel. Now, let's look at the three items of merchandise He offers to Laodicea. The first is "gold tried in the fire" (Revelation 3:18). What does this represent? Peter gives us a clue:

> For a season, if need be, ye are in heaviness through manifold temptations: That the trial of your faith, being much more precious than of gold that perisheth, though it be tried with fire, might be found unto praise and honour and glory at the appearing of Jesus Christ (1 Peter 1:6, 7).

"Gold tried in the fire" is simply "faith that has been purified of self." It is the faith of Jesus Christ, because Jesus' faith was purified by fire at Gethsemane and at the cross. In Gethsemane, Jesus prayed three times, "Father, if thou be willing, remove this cup from me: nevertheless not my will, but thine, be done" (Luke 22:42). He didn't allow self to have any part in His redemptive mission. Every trace of self was crucified in the life and death of Christ (see Luke 9:23).

When we first accept Christ, our faith is still egocentric. We accept Him either because we are afraid of the judgment or because we want to go to heaven. That is the normal experience of most Christians. But Christ wants to purify our faith of this egocentric motivation. He wants us to have what Paul calls "faith which worketh by love" (Galatians 5:6). That is the gold tried in the fire that the True Witness wants us to have.

"Faith and love are golden treasures, elements that are greatly wanting among God's people" (*Testimonies for the Church*, 3:255). Don't we have faith? Yes, but it is an egocentric faith. We must give it up for the faith that is motivated by *agape* love. We must exchange our self-centered faith for Christ's self-sacrificing faith. Ellen White says:

> The gold tried in the fire is faith that works by love. Only this can bring us into harmony with God. We may be active, we may do much work; but without love, such love as dwelt in the heart of Christ, we can never be numbered with the family of heaven (*Christ's Object Lessons*, 158).

We must be careful when we read such a statement that we don't read it only in the context of justification. Ellen White is writing here in terms of sanctification as well. Sanctification is the evidence of justification, and it must be reflected in us more and more. Without Christ's *agape* love, we can never truly reflect His character. There must be spiritual growth so that the very life of Christ will become our life. "The gold here recommended as having been tried in the fire is faith and love. It makes the heart rich; for it has been purged until it is

LAODICEA

pure, and the more it is tested the more brilliant is its luster" (*Testimonies for the Church*, 4:88).

So the gold Christ offers is "faith which worketh by love" (Galatians 5:6). It is a faith that has been purged of self. That is what the True Witness is offering us. He says, "I want to offer you My faith, which is motivated by pure love, in exchange for your faith, which is self-centered."

The second item Christ offers Laodicea is white clothing. This is the righteousness of Jesus—both imputed and imparted. But we need to be clear that it is His *imputed* righteousness that qualifies us, or gives us the title, for heaven—not His imputed righteousness *plus* His imparted righteousness. The righteousness that qualifies us for heaven was accomplished *for* us, but *outside* us, in the holy life and death of Christ. Imparted righteousness reproduces Christ's righteousness *within* us; it gives evidence that His righteousness has been imputed to us by faith and thus fits us for heaven. This is an important distinction because some teach that the righteousness that qualifies us for heaven is a combination of the imputed righteousness of Christ (justification) *plus* His imparted righteousness (sanctification).

Paul says, "What shall we say then? That the Gentiles, which followed not after righteousness, have attained to righteousness, even the righteousness which is of faith. But Israel, which followed after the law of righteousness, hath not attained to the law of righteousness" (Romans 9:30, 31). He presents two groups of people—Gentiles and Israel—and two methods of achieving righteousness—faith or law keeping. The Gentiles succeeded, and the Jews failed. Why? Because the Gentiles accepted Christ as their righteousness, while the Jews tried to become righteous through law keeping.

Paul is saying that there can be no mixture of self-righteousness and Christ our righteousness. It is either one or the other. The moment you accept Christ's righteousness, you must give up your own self-righteousness. The moment you uphold self-righteousness, Christ's

Laodicea is counseled

righteousness becomes an offense to you. Paul concludes, "Whosoever believeth on him [Christ] shall not be ashamed" (verse 33). Those who buy the white clothing will ensure that the shame of their nakedness will not appear (see Revelation 3:18). They will not be ashamed, because they will be clothed with the imputed righteousness of Christ, the only righteousness that will be able to stand perfect in the judgment. If we appear in the judgment in our own self-righteousness, we will appear naked, because God looks not only at what we have done, but at the motive for doing it. In fact, He is concerned primarily with motive. And self-righteousness is always motivated, or polluted, with self. It's true that our works (the imparted righteousness of Christ) will testify in the judgment that we have received His imputed righteousness, but they will not contribute in the least to our justification.

So the white clothing that the True Witness offers to Laodicea is the imputed and imparted righteousness of Christ. "The marriage of the Lamb is come," John writes, "and his wife hath made herself ready. And to her was granted that she should be arrayed in fine linen, clean and white: for the fine linen is the righteousness of saints" (Revelation 19:7, 8). Christ has been waiting for generations to reproduce His character in His bride so that she might be ready for the marriage.

Is the fine linen, the white clothing, something that the bride produces for herself? Does she make herself ready through self-effort? No! It *was granted* that she should be clothed in white raiment. Christ clothes His bride; she does not clothe herself. "The white raiment is purity of character, the righteousness of Christ imparted to the sinner. This is indeed a garment of heavenly texture that can be bought only of Christ for a life of willing obedience" (*Testimonies for the Church*, 4: 88). Here, Ellen White does not mean obedience in the sense of obedience to the law; "willing obedience" means being willing to say, "Not I, but Christ." It is an obedience of faith that manifests itself in obedience to all the commandments of God.

Finally, the True Witness offers us eye salve. In the Middle East during New Testament times, people didn't have sunglasses, of course. They used a black ointment to protect their eyes from the glare of the sun and to help them see without squinting in its harsh light. The eye salve is used as a symbol of the Holy Spirit opening our eyes. The Holy Spirit guides us into all truth (see John 16:13, 14). He is the only One who can open our eyes and show us our true condition—that our self-righteousness is like filthy rags. Ellen White writes, "The eyesalve is that wisdom and grace which enables us to discern between the evil and the good and to detect sin under any guise" (*Testimonies for the Church*, 4:88). Self-righteousness is actually sin, but it doesn't appear to be sinful. It looks good—until the eye salve allows us to see it in its true light.

Remember that the general context of the entire Laodicean message is "works." The key phrase is "I know thy works" (Revelation 3:15). Are Laodicea's works hot? Are they cold? They are neither; they are lukewarm. Christ wants our works to be hot. And they can be hot only through His imparted righteousness. He offers us His imputed righteousness so we may be clothed and not stand naked in the judgment. But He also offers us His imparted righteousness so that He may be fully reflected in us. This has to take place before the end can come (see Revelation 18:1).

> Again and again has the voice from heaven addressed you. Will you obey this voice? Will you heed the counsel of the True Witness to seek the gold tried in the fire, the white raiment, and the eyesalve? The gold is faith and love, the white raiment is the righteousness of Christ, the eyesalve is that spiritual discernment which will enable you to see the wiles of Satan and shun them, to detest sin and abhor it, to see truth and obey it (*Testimonies for the Church*, 5:233).

For this reason, God allows the last generation of Christians to go

Laodicea is counseled

through the time of trouble. It is part of the work of producing the righteous character of Christ in us; it is part of the process of reflecting the white clothing we have "bought" from Christ. Ellen White writes:

> Their [God's people's] affliction is great, the flames of the furnace seem about to consume them; but the Refiner will bring them forth as gold tried in the fire. God's love for His children during the period of their severest trial is as strong and tender as in the days of their sunniest prosperity; but it is needful to be placed in the furnace of fire; their earthliness must be consumed, that the image of Christ may be perfectly reflected (*The Great Controversy*, 621).

Notice that the time of trouble will be the real test of righteousness by faith, showing whether we have truly bought the pure white raiment of Christ. What will we have to give up in the time of trouble? We will have to abandon any attempt to hold on to self-righteousness, because the real issue in the great tribulation will be our faith (see Luke 18:8; Isaiah 54:5-8). This refining process does not secure salvation for us. Rather, its purpose is to demonstrate to the world that the gospel "is the power of God unto salvation" (Romans 1:16). Then God will declare to the world, "Here are My people who have the faith of Jesus. You can try them to the very limit. You cannot kill them, but you can test them." And as we are tested, what will appear is a faith motivated by self-sacrificing love. Our anchor in the time of trouble will not be our love for God, but God's love for us (see Romans 8:35-39). Our faith will lay hold on His love, which was manifested for sinners on the cross.

What held Jesus to the cross? Why didn't He come down and save Himself when taunted to do so? Wasn't He able to do that? Of course, He was able! But by faith He clung to the Father's love. As far as His

LAODICEA

feelings were concerned, He *felt* the Father had forsaken Him. But by faith He believed in the love of God that never fails (see 1 Corinthians 13:8). We need that kind of faith as well. Our faith, too, must be in God's love and His righteousness, which He has given us freely in Jesus Christ.

Notice how Ellen White describes the faith of Jesus tried by fire at the cross:

> Amid the awful darkness, apparently forsaken of God, Christ had drained the last dregs in the cup of human woe. In those dreadful hours He had relied upon the evidence of His Father's acceptance heretofore given Him. He was acquainted with the character of His Father; He understood His justice, His mercy, and His great love. By faith He rested in Him whom it had ever been His joy to obey. And as in submission He committed Himself to God, the sense of the loss of His Father's favor was withdrawn. By faith, Christ was victor (*The Desire of Ages*, 756).

Christ comes to each of us and says, "Will you please buy? Will you please give up your own self-evaluation that has deceived you so badly? Will you give up all your spiritual successes and all those badges that the church has given you for your great efforts? Are you willing to consider all that as rubbish in exchange for My righteousness?"

We must each choose. I know the choice I have made. I have discovered that the righteousness which can qualify me for heaven is not a successful ministry. It is not the number of people I baptized in Africa. The only righteousness that can qualify me for heaven is Christ's righteousness. May God help us, individually and as a church, to buy the gold, the white clothing and the eye salve that will make it possible for us to reflect the character of Christ fully in these last days!

CHAPTER 6

LAODICEA
is rebuked

As many as I love, I rebuke and chasten: be zealous therefore, and repent.
REVELATION 3:19

About three or four weeks after I arrived in America in 1982, a large evangelistic effort was held in the district where I was working. All the pastors in that area were required to participate. It was a new experience for me. The evangelist had three screens and thirteen projectors, all connected to a computer. Coming from Africa, I was amazed to see how this computer worked and how all these thirteen projectors were so wonderfully synchronized! I said to myself, "If we had this equipment in Africa, maybe we would baptize thousands of people!"

But in spite of all the gadgets, we baptized only twenty-six persons at the end of those meetings. Fifteen of these had already been prepared for baptism, even before the meetings began. So at the close of the meetings, I said to myself, "With all the money we spent and all the equipment we had, the results were very poor."

LAODICEA

I am convinced that before we will see Pentecostal results follow our preaching, there will first have to be a Pentecostal work done in us. In 1888, when the message of righteousness by faith came to this church in a strong way, Ellen White said that the work of that message was to lay "the glory of man in the dust" (*Testimonies to Ministers*, 456). Unless that takes place, unless we can say from the heart, "Not I, but Christ," He cannot take over completely and finish His work.

It would be wonderful if the Laodicean message had ended with the counsel in verse 18. Unfortunately, there is more. Like the Jews, we have been stiff-necked and rebellious. So the Lord has had to take an additional step. That step is found in verse 19: "As many as I love, I rebuke and chasten: be zealous therefore, and repent." Ellen White has written: "The testimony of the True Witness has not been half heeded. The solemn testimony upon which the destiny of the church hangs has been lightly esteemed, if not entirely disregarded. This testimony must work deep repentance, and all that truly receive it will obey it and be purified" (*Testimonies for the Church*, 1:181).

I am convinced that the reason the second coming has been delayed is not because of an *unfinished* work but because of our *independent* work. I'm not talking about independent groups that continue to take shots at the church—although that is a problem. I'm talking about our efforts to arouse church members and finish the work in our own strength. Bigger budgets, better quality printing, more sophisticated gadgets, and new programs will never finish the work—as important as all these may be.

Let's examine, then, the rebuke the True Witness gives Laodicea. The first thing we notice is how He begins: "As many as I love I rebuke . . ." Thank God, He doesn't rebuke us in anger but out of a deep, loving concern for Laodicea. This has always been true in God's dealings with His people. "For whom the Lord loveth he chasteneth, and scourgeth every son whom he receiveth. If ye endure chastening, God dealeth with you as sons; for what son is he whom the father

Laodicea is rebuked

chasteneth not?" (Hebrews 12:6, 7).

However, some of us have had human fathers who chastened us in anger. They wanted to give vent to their feelings. Sometimes human parents discipline unjustly or excessively or from the wrong motives. God, however, disciplines us "for our profit, that we might be partakers of his holiness" (verse 10).

In spite of our failures, God loves us. God's love is unconditional. So the first thing to realize about the rebuke Christ gives Laodicea is that it is based in His unconditional love. His love causes Him to rebuke and chasten us.

A rebuke usually refers to a *verbal* reproof or correction. For example, Jesus rebuked Peter once, saying, "Get thee behind me, Satan" (Mark 8:33). He rebuked the eleven disciples for their unbelief (see Mark 16:14). He rebuked those who were criticizing Mary (see John 12:7). Through the prophets, God sent rebukes to His Old Testament people many times. He has also sent rebukes to His church today through Ellen White. In one such rebuke, she wrote:

> Oh, for a religious awakening! The angels of God are going from church to church, doing their duty; and Christ is knocking at the door of your hearts for entrance. But the means that God has devised to awaken the church to a sense of their spiritual destitution have not been regarded. The voice of the True Witness has been heard in reproof, but has not been obeyed. Men have chosen to follow their own way instead of God's way because self was not crucified in them. Thus the light has had but little effect upon minds and hearts (*Testimonies for the Church*, 5:719, 720).

If we still don't listen even after He has rebuked us verbally, God has to take a further step to correct the problem, a much tougher measure. Those He loves, He first rebukes. But if that is ineffective, He says, "I will have to chasten you as well." The word *chasten* means " to

LAODICEA

punish." This punishment could be physical; it could be economic. It is something that God allows to happen to you for the purpose of correcting or disciplining you. But remember that even His chastening issues from and is administered in love.

The Babylonian captivity is an example of how God chastens. For years, He tried to get Israel to turn from idolatry, but they would not listen. He rebuked them through prophet after prophet. Finally, as a last resort, God said, "You won't listen to rebuke, so I will chastise you. I will allow a foreign, pagan government to take you captives." It was His final resort because Israel would not listen to earlier rebukes. And if we refuse to listen to God, He will chastise us as well. I don't know what form it might take. It could be a financial collapse; it could be something else that would knock the props from under society. Our whole social system might come under attack. The Babylonian captivity was devastating to the Jews. But remember, God's chastisements are an evidence of His love and concern. "As many as I love . . . I chasten" (Revelation 3:19).

Jesus uses the illustration of the vine and its branches to symbolize His relationship to us and ours to Him (see John 15:1-8). He wants to produce fruit in us, and therefore He has to prune the branches. Now, pruning is painful, but it has a beautiful purpose. And God hopes the result is beautiful as well—a rich harvest of fruit in our lives. This disciplining, refining, pruning process is apparent throughout Scripture from beginning to end. God disciplines in love in order to reproduce His love and His righteousness in us.

In the context of Christ's message to Laodicea, what is the purpose of His rebukes and His chastening? It is that we will repent and be zealous of good works. Notice that the words *rebuke* and *chasten* are in the present tense. God will continue to use these methods until they achieve the desired result. It's interesting that the word John uses for *zealous* is from the same root as the word *hot* used earlier in describing the works God wishes Laodicea possessed. God is saying, then: "I want

Laodicea is rebuked

you to get hot in terms of your works by repenting and becoming zealous."

The word *repent* means simply "a change of mind." That's what the Greek word means—a change of mind or direction. It's a U-turn. I was driving along the freeway one morning going to the airport, when all at once I discovered that my airline ticket was still lying on the counter at home! I had forgotten it! I made a U-turn on the freeway as quickly as possible. That's what repentance is. When God asks us to repent, He's saying, "I want you to make a U-turn from being self-centered to being God-centered, from depending on self to depending on Me."

Remember the conflict between our evaluation of our own spiritual condition and Christ's evaluation of us. Because works of the law have deceived us, we think that we are "rich, and increased with goods, and have need of nothing." But Christ assures us that we are "wretched, and miserable, and poor, and blind, and naked" (Revelation 3:17). Here are two conflicting opinions—ours and Christ's. To repent means to give up our opinion of ourselves and to accept Christ's opinion of us. If we don't do this, we will have to learn the hard way, as Peter did, that Christ is right and we are wrong.

At the Passover feast, when Christ instituted the Lord's Supper, Peter had to learn through chastisement that Jesus knew him better than he knew himself. After supper, Jesus turned to Peter and said, "Simon, Simon, behold, Satan hath desired to have you, that he may sift you as wheat: But I have prayed for thee, that thy faith fail not: and when thou art converted, strengthen thy brethren" (Luke 22:31, 32). In the Middle East, farmers sifted wheat by placing the threshed grain on a flat tray of woven grass. Then they threw the contents into the air; the wind would blow away the lighter chaff while the grain would fall back onto the tray. "Pay attention, Peter," Jesus warned. "Satan wants to treat you like chaff and blow you away, to separate you from Me."

Satan was trying to destroy Peter's faith. That is always his plan.

LAODICEA

When he discourages us, when he makes life difficult for us, he always has a single objective: to destroy our faith. Notice Peter's response to Jesus' warning. "Lord, I am ready to go with thee, both into prison, and to death" (verse 33).

Peter was so sure that Jesus was wrong. "What on earth are You talking about, Lord? I fail You? My faith fail? You're mistaken, Lord. I don't need Your prayers. I'll never fail."

Did Peter fail, or didn't he? He certainly did. Just as Jesus had predicted, Peter denied Him three times and with cursing and swearing. In Jewish thinking, to deny God with cursing was to commit the unpardonable sin. God could not forgive such a person, for he had reached the point of no return. So when Peter cursed and denied the Lord, he no doubt felt that there was no hope for him.

But did Jesus abandon Peter because of his sin and his spiritual arrogance? No. Even though Peter failed Him, Jesus didn't forsake him. After the resurrection, before Jesus saw Peter, even before He had appeared to any of the disciples, the angel at the tomb told Mary, "Go your way, tell his [Jesus'] disciples *and Peter* that he goeth before you into Galilee: there shall ye see him" (Mark 16:7, emphasis supplied). If Mary had told Jesus' friends, "The angel said that Jesus will appear to the disciples," Peter would have thought, *That doesn't include me; I've denied him, and there is no hope for me.* But Jesus wanted Peter to know that he was specifically included, that he was still a disciple, even though he had failed so miserably.

That is a lesson we need to know today as well. There are many today who say that the Seventh-day Adventist Church no longer belongs to Christ because it has failed and become Babylon. Peter's experience tells us that God is patient. He has been rebuking us, and to some degree He has been chastising us. We have had some crises as a church, but nothing to compare with what is coming if we continue to refuse to listen. But in spite of His rebukes and His chastening, Jesus does not abandon us. "As many as I love, I rebuke and chasten: be

Laodicea is rebuked

zealous therefore, and repent" (Revelation 3:19).

Peter had to learn the hard way to trust Jesus and distrust self. Peter had failed his Lord and denied Him three times. But now he was broken. His spiritual arrogance was gone. He had repented. When they met later on the seashore after the resurrection, Jesus didn't say, "I told you so, Peter; now you must suffer." Instead, He forgave him and reinstated him. It's true that He put Peter through an embarrassing, bitter experience in order to chasten him. Twice, Jesus asked Peter, "Do you love [*agape*] Me?" And Peter replied twice, "You know that I love [*philos*] You" (see John 21:15ff). There is a play on words in these verses that doesn't come across in English.

Jesus was asking, "Peter, do you love Me unconditionally?"

And Peter responded, "Lord, You know that I love You," but he used the word that means fluctuating, unreliable, human love. In other words, Peter was saying, "Lord, You knew all along how frail and unreliable my love is. I didn't believe You, but now I admit You were right, and I was wrong. I repent."

Then the third time, Jesus switched to *philos* and said, "Peter, do you love [philos] Me?" In other words, "Is this the only kind of love you have for Me, Peter? This unreliable, human kind of love?"

Peter was hurt and embarrassed, but he was converted now. He admitted his hurt. He said, "Lord, You know everything. You know that I love [philos] You. That's all the love I'm capable of in myself." And Jesus was not discouraged by Peter's response. He said in effect, "Now that you are converted, I can use you. Feed My sheep; feed My lambs."

God cannot fully use us until we have lost confidence in self. When God's people put self aside and make room for the Holy Spirit to take over, the work will be finished. That is what God is looking for. We need to repent. We need to repent of our pride—whether it's individual pride or denominational pride. We need to admit that we have failed God. God says to us, just as Paul told the Jews, "You claim to know the truth. You claim to understand what is right and what is

LAODICEA

wrong from God's law, but you have blasphemed the name of God in the eyes of the world" (see Romans 2:17-24).

Recently, a church member brought a document to my house. It was a survey taken by a firm that polls society on various issues. This survey was an attempt to determine the feelings of the American public toward religion, and specifically toward Seventh-day Adventists and their message. The survey was conducted in Pittsburgh, Pennsylvania; Des Moines, Iowa; and Seattle, Washington. In Pittsburgh, where Roman Catholics are predominant, people knew very little about Adventists; they hardly listened to us. Des Moines, with a mixture of Protestants and Roman Catholics, had a little more awareness. Seattle, where the majority of people are not interested in religion and do not attend any church, knew virtually nothing about Adventists and weren't interested. Nonchurch attenders in all three cities said, "We don't need religion. People have a certain amount of goodness built into them. What we need to do is to improve our human relationships by building on that goodness."

Seattle residents were revolted by Adventist literature. Of certain brochures, they said, "The emphasis is fear; they present a God who is out to punish people." They felt the pictures looked almost pornographic. Very few found our literature appealing. It was, in fact, quite devastating to find out what people thought about us. So while we are boasting among ourselves of our spiritual riches, the general public has a very low opinion of us—according to this survey.

We only need to mix with other Christians to discover that many of them also have a low opinion of Seventh-day Adventists. They often see us as a proud, self-righteous people who feel spiritually superior to other Christians. When I was a chaplain at Nairobi University in Kenya, I worked with chaplains of various denominations. I was the only Adventist. One day, a fellow chaplain told me, "You know, you're the first chaplain from the Adventist Church who has been willing to mix with us. The others gave us the impression we were untouchables."

Laodicea is rebuked

A Calvinist scholar in Grand Rapids, Michigan, has written a book about Adventism. He wrote it as a textbook on the four major cults in America. One of the issues he deals with is Seventh-day Adventism's claim to be God's remnant church. He says that although Adventists admit that there are true Christians in other churches, they insist that only they are the "remnant." He feels that Adventists believe they are the only ones who are faithful to God and that all others are second-class Christians.

But even these perceptions are not our biggest problem. The fact that society has a negative view of us is not the main issue. The world had a negative view of the early Christian church as well. The main issue is that *Christ* has a negative opinion of our spiritual achievements. He is saying, "I want you to repent. I want you to give up your opinions about yourself. I want you to take your righteousness and lay it in the dust. Accept My white clothing—My righteousness. Accept the eye salve that will enable you to see clearly." Are we willing to say, "God, You are right. We have failed to reveal Your character of love to the world"? Are we willing to repent?

Ellen White challenges us:

> The Lord calls for a renewal of the straight testimony borne in years past. He calls for a renewal of spiritual life. The spiritual energies of His people have long been torpid, but there is to be a resurrection from apparent death. By prayer and confession of sin we must clear the King's highway. As we do this, the power of the Spirit will come to us. We need the Pentecostal energy. This will come, for the Lord has promised to send His Spirit as the all-conquering power (*Gospel Workers*, 307, 308).

Here, there is no evidence of accusing the church, "You are Babylon!" Instead, there is a plea for us to repent, to turn around. Not just Peter, but each of the disciples at the Lord's Supper were full of confidence

LAODICEA

in themselves. Each of them disagreed with Christ when He said, "All of you will forsake Me." They were full of self, and as a result they were always jealous of one another. Even at the Lord's Supper they were competing to be the greatest in the kingdom (see Luke 22). They each wanted to be the prime minister or the finance minister. Their focus was egocentric.

We have a similar situation in the church whenever we have an election. We join factions, and those who are close friends of a particular person will say, "When you get into power, I hope you will give me a high position." The disciples had this mentality. Then came the cross, and their hopes were dashed to pieces. They said, "We thought He was the One who was going to restore the kingdom and establish it. But now He is dead." They were downcast, and their faith had failed.

But forty days later, these same disciples were of one heart and mind in the upper room. Self had been crucified; they had experienced deep repentance. The cross had done its work in their lives, turning them from self to Jesus. We need this same experience. Self must be crucified. It is painful, but God demands it. When we say in deep repentance, "God, I admit that in me there is nothing good. I admit that in my human nature I am capable of any sin, no matter how gross. Cleanse me. Change my heart and my life"—when we have this experience then we will understand what the disciples felt at Pentecost. All who belong to Christ, says Paul, have crucified the flesh with its desires and passions (see Galatians 5:24).

When I see what Hitler did to the Jews or what Idi Amin did to his own people in Uganda and realize that my sinful human nature is no different from theirs, then I must acknowledge that given the right set of circumstances, I am capable of doing just what these men did. We look at the Holocaust and say, "How could the Germans do that?" They could practice these atrocities because they turned their backs on God. When Hitler repudiated God, then unrighteousness came naturally. And when this country turns its back on God, we will find that we are capable of doing exactly what Hitler did. In fact, we are doing it now to a certain degree. When we condone abortion on demand and kill millions of unwanted babies each year, are we really different from those who killed some six million Jews in Nazi Germany?

It's crucial that we repent as the True Witness calls on us to do. We should pray that God will not have to chastise us anymore. We need to surrender to His testimony and admit that we are wretched and miserable and poor and blind and naked. We need to admit that He is right and that our only hope is to accept the heavenly merchandise through deep, heartfelt repentance. Only then can we be filled with His Spirit and power. Then we will turn the world upside down, as the early disciples did.

During her lifetime, Ellen White pleaded for and hoped to see this repentance, but did not. Notice these two statements:

> The message to Laodicea has not accomplished that zealous repentance among God's people which I expected to see, and my perplexity of mind has been great (*Testimonies for the Church*, 1:185).

> The same disobedience and failure that were seen in the Jewish church have characterized in a greater degree the people who have had this great light from heaven in the last messages of warning. Shall we, like them, squander our opportunities and privileges until God shall permit oppression and persecution to come upon us? (ibid., 5:456, 457).

God doesn't give up easily. He isn't through with us yet. He is patient. Those who accuse the church of being Babylon are wrong. It is true we have drifted far from God's blueprint. We have failed to lift up Christ as we should. But God has not forsaken us. He still intends to fill us with His righteousness so that the world can see "Christ in us,

LAODICEA

the hope of glory" (see Colossians 1:27).
    How long will we keep the world—and God—waiting?

CHAPTER 7

LAODICEA
must repent

Be zealous therefore, and repent.
REVELATION 3:19

Bible repentance is always specific. When Peter preached at Pentecost, telling the Jews that they had crucified the Son of God, the people cried out, "What shall we do?"

Peter replied, "Repent" (Acts 2:37, 38). Specifically, they needed to repent in terms of the crucifixion of the Messiah.

As we saw in the last chapter, repentance means "a change of mind" or "a change of direction." In modern terms, we would describe it as a U-turn. This can be a physical turning around or a change of the mind.

In what sense, then, is Christ asking Laodicea to repent? When we look at the specific context of His message to Laodicea, we see that He is calling on us to repent in two areas that are related.

First, we need to have a change of mind in regard to the conflicting evaluations of our spiritual condition brought out in Revelation 3:17. *We* say that we are rich and increased with goods and have need of

LAODICEA

nothing." *Christ* says we are "wretched, and miserable, and poor, and blind, and naked." We need to change our minds and agree that Christ is right and we are wrong. We need to repent of our wrong self-evaluation.

Second, we need to have a change in direction from our works of the law to the works of faith Jesus describes in verse 18. This means to make a U-turn from our own self-righteousness to Christ's righteousness. One of the most difficult things for a person to do—even a Christian—is to repent of self-righteousness. It's one thing to repent of our sins; it's another thing altogether to repent of our self-righteousness, because these are things that look good, things that we are proud of doing!

Jesus told the Jewish nation, "It will be easier for Nineveh in the judgment than for you" (see Matthew 12:41). Why? Because the people of Nineveh were guilty of terrible sins. They recognized that they were sinners and repented. But did the Jews repent? No. Why not? Because they didn't realize that they needed to repent. They were filled with a sense of all the "good" things they did. They needed to repent of self-righteousness, and this is extremely difficult to do.

Let's look at another case study of repentance from self-righteousness. This one may create a bit of a problem in your mind, because I want to give a nontraditional interpretation to a familiar person in the Bible. Let's look at the story of a man who appears in the oldest book of the Bible—the book of Job.

I've wrestled with the book of Job for a long time. I could never see why God allowed Satan to mistreat Job so badly and why Job had to go through all those terrible crises without any purpose other than to prove to Satan that God was right. To me, that didn't seem to be enough; the whole story somehow didn't seem to fit with what I knew of God's character. Then one day I was reading *The Desire of Ages*, and I came across these words: "The history of Job had shown that suffering is inflicted by Satan, and is overruled by God for purposes of mercy"

Laodicea must repent

(471). But Ellen White didn't say exactly what that merciful purpose was in Job's case. The only way I could find out was to read and study and wrestle with the book of Job for myself.

When I began studying the book closely, I discovered that Job himself had a problem. At first, it was hard to accept what I was learning, because it completely contradicted what I had always understood about Job. I had always had the picture that we get from the very first verse of the book. It says that Job "was blameless and upright, and one who feared God and shunned evil" (Job 1:1, NKJV). This description of Job is repeated in verse 8 when God is having a dialogue with Satan. " 'Have you considered My servant Job, that there is none like him on the earth, a blameless and upright man, one who fears God and shuns evil?' " (NKJV).

And Satan replies, "Yes, but he does all this because You have built a hedge around him. Remove Your protection, and give him into my hands. You'll see what he will do then. He will deny You and reject You. He will turn his back on You" (see verses 9-11).

So God said, "You can have him. Everything he possesses is in your power, but you can't touch his body. You can't kill him." Immediately, Satan set out to destroy everything Job had—including his children (see verses 13-19). How would you react after losing your children and everything you owned? Job "tore his robe and shaved his head, and he fell to the ground and worshiped. And he said, 'Naked I came from my mother's womb, and naked shall I return there. The Lord gave, and the Lord has taken away; blessed be the name of the Lord!' " (verses 20, 21, NKJV).

Job didn't turn his back on God. He was a righteous person. But this is the crucial question: Was his righteousness the righteousness of faith, or was it the righteousness of works? We need to look closely at his experience in order to determine the answer to this question, because I believe we will find in Job's story clear similarities to our own situation as Laodicea.

LAODICEA

In chapter 2, God and Satan have a second conversation regarding Job. Satan says to God, "All right, Job hasn't rejected You yet. But let me touch *him*—not just his possessions or his children. Let me get his own body in my hands; he will deny You then!"

And God replied, "Go ahead. He is in your hands, but you can't kill him."

Satan caused Job to break out in terrible boils from head to foot. At this point, Job's wife had had enough. " 'Do you still hold to *your* integrity?' " she asked. " 'Curse God and die!' " (Job 2:9, NKJV, emphasis supplied). But Job didn't listen. "In all this Job did not sin with his lips" (verse 10, NKJV).

Three new characters enter the story, the so-called friends of Job—Eliphaz, Bildad, and Zophar. The arguments of these "comforters" are typical of the Eastern mentality regarding human suffering. All through the book, they are arguing that Job's intense sufferings are the result of some secret sin in his life. "You wouldn't be in this condition, Job, if there wasn't something wrong in your spiritual life. God wouldn't be punishing you like this otherwise."

Does God punish us like that? Does He cause us to suffer physically for our sins? No. We need to remember that the arguments of Job's friends are based on human reasoning, not biblical truth. That is why God rebukes them in the end. They were misrepresenting His character. But the important element in this story is Job's reaction to all this. He doesn't reject their reasoning regarding punishment for sin, but he defends his righteousness. That is why Job is so puzzled. Like his friends, he, too, believes that the wicked will suffer and the righteous prosper in this life. Yet he is suffering in spite of being righteous! That is what Job cannot understand.

" 'Teach me, and I will hold my tongue; cause me to understand wherein I have erred. How forceful are right words! But what does your arguing prove?. . . Is there injustice on my tongue?' " (Job 6:24, 25, 30, NKJV). He defends his righteousness before his friends. He is saying, "Where have I gone wrong? Show me what sin you are accusing me of. I am blameless, even though I am suffering."

By the time we reach chapter 10, Job is defending his righteousness to God Himself. "I will say to God, 'Do not condemn me; show me why You contend with me. . . . You know that I am not wicked' " (verses 2, 7, NKJV). Later, he pleads with God to show him his sins. Actually, Job is quite confident that his righteousness is perfect. "God," Job says, "these friends of mine are accusing me of some secret sin. Show me where I am wrong. I would really like to know what my sin is." Of course, Job was convinced of his righteousness; he didn't think he was guilty of sin.

Was there some sin in Job's life that was the cause of his suffering? No. But did Job have a problem? Yes.

Job continues to insist on his own righteousness and to defend himself against the accusations of his friends. They keep saying, "Job, you must have some secret sin in your life; look how you're suffering!"

And Job argues back, "No. I have not sinned. I have kept God's commandments; I have held to my integrity." Notice what he says in chapter 23. " 'My foot has held fast to His steps; I have kept His way and not turned aside. I have not departed from the commandment of His lips; I have treasured the words of His mouth more than my necessary food' " (verses 11, 12, NKJV).

Does this sound like a man who has been justified by faith? Or does it sound like a man who is confident of his own righteousness, who is self-righteous?

By chapter 31, Job is strongly defending his own righteousness. He calls upon God to judge him. "Let me be weighed in a just balance, that God may know my integrity" (verse 6, NKJV). He goes on to list the good works he has habitually done—fed the hungry, clothed the naked, cared for orphans and widows, and opened his home to the homeless. This chapter is Job's final argument against the accusations of his three friends. "So these three men ceased answering Job, because he was righteous in his own eyes" (Job 32:1, NKJV).

This was Job's problem—he was righteous in his own eyes. He was sincere; he was honest. But he had a problem he didn't recognize. The book of Job is a historical account of God's first lesson on righteousness by faith. Let's see how this is so.

After Job's three friends quit arguing with him, a fourth man steps in—Elihu. He asks Job, "Do you think this is right? Do you say, 'My righteousness is more than God's'?" (Job 35:2, NKJV). Elihu has put his finger on an important point. He isn't trying to convince Job that his problem is sin, as did the other three friends. He is trying to convince Job that his problem is self-righteousness. And he continues this argument until chapter 38, when God steps in at last to settle the matter. If you read from chapter 38 to the end of the book, you'll find that God rebukes Job's three friends for their mistaken theology. They argued, "Job, you must be a sinner. The fact that you are suffering is proof of sin in your life because God punishes those who do bad things." And God says, "No. You're wrong. Suffering is not always proof of God's punishing of sin." So Job was right to reject the argument of his three friends.

But God also rebukes Job. "Who is this who darkens counsel by words without knowledge? Now prepare yourself like a man; I will question you, and you shall answer Me" (Job 38:2, 3, NKJV). God rebukes Job for his self-righteous attitude.

And notice that Job repents. "Then Job answered the Lord and said: 'Behold, I am vile; what shall I answer You? I lay my hand over my mouth' " (Job 40:3, 4, NKJV). God's words silenced Job's pretensions to righteousness. Job's problem was self-righteousness. His attitude was that of the rich young ruler who came to Jesus saying, "All these things have I kept from my youth up" (Matthew 19:20). Job was so focused on all the good things he did and the lack of sinful things in his life that he couldn't recognize the source of his righteousness was self rather than God. But when he came face to face with God, he admitted, " 'I have uttered what I did not understand, things too wonderful for me, which I did not know. . . . Therefore I abhor myself, and repent in dust and ashes' " (Job 42:3, 6, NKJV).

What was it that Job had not understood? He had not understood that his self-righteousness was mere filthy rags in God's sight. But when he came face to face with his self-righteous condition, he abhorred himself and repented in dust and ashes. That is what Laodicea needs to do as well. Have we come to that point?

Repentance from self-righteousness is terribly painful because we have to swallow our pride—our spiritual pride. The things we have looked to as evidences of our goodness, we have to see as monuments to self. It was hard for Job to admit he had a problem in his spiritual life. It was hard for Peter to repent of his own opinion. It was hard for Paul to give up his righteousness of the law. But each of these realized that God was right and that He was their only hope. Are we prepared to take that hard step—both as individuals and as a denomination?

God didn't enjoy putting Job through this crisis. But Job had a lesson to learn, and this drastic method was the only way to teach him. God allowed Satan to touch Job for a purpose—to correct him of his self-righteousness. When the lesson was complete and Job was fully converted, God was able to bless him again. He restored his health, his possessions, and his children.

Christ's message to Laodicea will also produce a shaking—a traumatic time for God's people. I don't know exactly how God will chastise us today, but I do know that His purpose will be the same as was His purpose for Job. Out of that shaking time will come a people who will have repented of their self-righteousness, a people who will have turned to Christ's righteousness fully and completely, a people who will abhor self and the righteousness it produces. The ultimate end of true Christianity is that the Christian rejoices in Christ and has no confidence in the flesh (see Philippians 3:3).

Have you ever wondered why God allows His people to be harassed

LAODICEA

after probation has closed? When probation closes, there can be no change in status. God has said, "He that is righteous, let him be righteous still: and he that is holy, let him be holy still" (Revelation 22:11). Those who are righteous by faith will remain so until the end; those who have rejected Christ will remain in that condition. Why, then, does God allow His righteous people to go through a time of terrible crisis *after* the close of probation—a crisis the like of which has never been experienced by any previous generation? Is He simply trying to prove a point? Is He just proving to the universe that these people will remain faithful to Him, no matter what He throws at them?

This statement from *The Great Controversy* helps us understand:

> Their [God's people's] affliction is great, the flames of the furnace seem about to consume them; but the Refiner will bring them forth as gold tried in the fire. God's love for His children during the period of their severest trial is as strong and tender as in the days of their sunniest prosperity; but it is needful for them to be placed in the furnace of fire; their earthliness must be consumed, that the image of Christ may be perfectly reflected (621).

When you are going through a crisis, it doesn't mean that God loves you any less. God's *agape* love never changes; it is eternal, unconditional, changeless (see Jeremiah 31:3). So the time of terrible trial following the close of probation doesn't indicate that God is not concerned about what happens to His people, any more than Job's experience showed a lack of concern on God's part for him. Self must be consumed so that the image of Jesus Christ may be reproduced in our lives. The world desperately needs to see Christ, but it cannot see Him in you or me unless every particle of self has been crucified. That is why God allows us to go through the refining process now, and that is why He will allow His people to go through the time of crisis following probation's close.

Laodicea must repent

In the time of trouble, Satan will point us to our feelings. Even after probation closes, we will still *feel* sinful. Even after probation closes, we will still *feel* that we aren't good enough to be saved. But the question is not how we feel. The question is: "Who is our righteousness?" The answer must be: "Christ." Every bit of self, every taint of earthliness must be consumed. We cannot look to ourselves or our experience. Christ can be fully reproduced in us only when we have said goodbye to self completely.

In this, as in all other aspects of our lives, Christ is our example. How was it possible for Him—not as God, but in our humanity, which He assumed—to perfectly reveal His Father? Paul gives us the steps in Philippians, chapter 2 and holds Christ up to us as our example. He says:

> Let this mind [attitude] be in you, which was also in Christ Jesus: Who, being in the form of God, thought it not robbery to be equal with God: But made himself of no reputation, and took upon him the form of a servant, and was made in the likeness of men: And being found in fashion as a man, he humbled himself, and became obedient unto death, even the death of the cross (verses 5-8).

The Greek word in verse 6 translated "equal" means "absolute sameness." Paul is saying that Jesus was one with the Father, equally divine in every regard. It was not sin for Him to make Himself equal with the Father. But instead, He emptied Himself. He didn't cling to His equality with the Father. He totally emptied Himself, gave up all His divine prerogatives, and became a slave! What condescension!

When Christ emptied Himself of self, who took over? His mind wasn't a vacuum. Luke gives us the answer. "Jesus being full of the Holy Ghost returned from Jordan, and was led by the Spirit" (Luke 4:1). When Jesus emptied Himself of self, He was filled with the Spirit.

LAODICEA

During His earthly mission, He was walking in the Spirit. That is what Paul admonishes us to do as well (see Romans 8:1, 4; Galatians 5:16). It was the Holy Spirit who controlled Jesus, and that is why He could reveal the Father perfectly.

Through the Spirit, Christ was totally dependent on His Father. He told His disciples, "Verily, verily, I say unto you, The Son can do nothing of himself, but what he seeth the Father do. . . . I can of mine own self do nothing" (John 5:19, 30). And just as Christ was totally dependent on His Father, so we are to be totally dependent on Christ. "Without me," He says, "ye can do nothing" (John 15:5). "As the living Father hath sent me, and I live by the Father: so he that eateth me, even he shall live by me" (John 6:57). It is not our righteousness that the world needs to see; it is Christ's righteousness.

Throughout His ministry on earth, Jesus repeated that He lived by the power of His Father, that the works He performed were done by the power of His Father (see John 10:32, 37, 38; 14:9-11). The same is true with us today; we must be clear about that. There is a great temptation for pastors today, in this modern age of education and an emphasis on academics, to present our own ideas. This is not feeding God's people. God must speak through our preaching of the Word, or the message is meaningless.

So God calls on Laodicea to repent. Specifically, He calls on us to repent of our false self-evaluation. We are *not* rich and increased with goods, and we need to admit it and repent. He calls on us to repent of our works of the law—our self-righteousness. We must move from works of law to works of faith, from self-righteousness to Christ's righteousness.

Now that we have seen what Christ is asking of us in terms of repentance, what will be our response? Our problem is that we are not guilty of gross sins. Like Job, our problem is that self-righteousness has deceived us. Do we need to repent of self-righteousness? Yes. It is crucial that we do so, and God will do everything in His power to help

Laodicea must repent

us. He will rebuke us first, as He does Laodicea. Then He will chastise us if necessary, as He did Job.

To what extent will He chastise us? I don't know, but if we look at Job's experience, we realize the chastisement can take drastic forms. Job lost his children, his possessions, his health, and almost his life itself. But God didn't allow these calamities to come to Job because He was angry with him or in order to justify Himself to Satan. He did it out of love. He knew that Job needed to learn this important lesson for his eternal good. And Job did learn the lesson. He did repent. He said, "God, You are right, and I am nothing." May God give us the wisdom to follow in Job's steps.

God has told us what His goal is for our lives: "I will dwell in them, and walk in them; and I will be their God, and they shall be my people" (2 Corinthians 6:16). This is the precious covenant, the "new covenant," that God wants to make with us. It is His promise to dwell in us through the Holy Spirit, just as the Spirit totally controlled Jesus during His earthly life.

> Love is the basis of godliness. Whatever the profession; no man has pure love to God unless he has unselfish love for his brother. But we can never come into possession of this spirit by trying to love others. What is needed is the love of Christ [*agape*] in the heart. When self is merged in Christ, love springs forth spontaneously. The completeness of Christian character is attained when the impulse to help and bless others springs constantly from within—when the sunshine of heaven fills the heart and is revealed in the countenance (*Christ's Object Lessons*, 384).

He wants to fulfill this promise in our lives; He wants to fulfill this promise in our church. And when that happens, the whole earth will be lightened with God's glory, and the end will come. But that cannot happen until we repent of our self-righteousness.

CHAPTER 8

LAODICEA
must open the door

Behold, I stand at the door, and knock: if any man hear my voice, and open the door, I will come in to him, and will sup with him, and he with me.
REVELATION 3:20

We have seen in previous chapters that Christ is calling on Laodicea to repent; that is her greatest need. She needs to turn from her own self-righteousness, which is based on works of the law, and embrace Christ's righteousness, which is based on works of faith. We have also seen that this change is one of the most difficult things for a Christian to do, because works of the law look so good outwardly. To repent from obvious sins is one thing, but to repent from what appear to be good deeds is something else altogether.

Some may ask at this point, "How can a person tell what is Christ's righteousness and what is self-righteousness? Works of the law closely resemble works of faith outwardly. How can we distinguish one from the other?"

It's true that the *actions* may appear to be the same. But the person

LAODICEA

who is operating from the basis of faith and the righteousness of Christ will always have the attitude that there is nothing good in himself or herself. There is no boasting, inwardly or outwardly, when Christ is living in us by faith. We recognize that it is Christ who deserves all the credit and praise. Our attitude is always, "I am chief of sinners" (1 Timothy 1:15).

So it is clear that Christ is calling on us, as Laodicea, to repent of our self-righteousness and accept by faith the righteousness that He offers freely. But how do we do this? What response does He expect of us?

The answer lies in these words to Laodicea. "Behold, I stand at the door, and knock: if any man hear my voice, and open the door, I will come in to him, and will sup with him, and he with me" (Revelation 3:20). The imagery of knocking at the door and asking to come in is reminiscent of the Song of Solomon. "It is the voice of my beloved that knocketh, saying, Open to me, my sister, my love" (Song of Solomon 5:2). Many Christians are uncomfortable with the Song of Solomon. Some even consider it to be biblical pornography and feel it shouldn't be in the Bible. But it is written for spiritually minded people and reveals God's great desire for a close, intimate relationship with His people. And that is what Christ is pleading for here in His message to Laodicea as well. He wants to bond with us in a relationship as close as that bonding that occurs between husband and wife—the two shall become one flesh.

When Christ says, "Behold, I stand at the door and knock," it sounds as though He is standing outside the door to our hearts, knocking and asking for admittance. And if He is *outside*, it implies that we are unconverted. Is Christ speaking here to the unconverted?

No. He has already identified Laodicea as His people—His church. These are not unconverted people; they belong to Him. What does He mean, then, when He asks us to open the door and allow Him to enter?

Laodicea must open the door

Christ is saying, "I am left on the outside when it comes to your works." That is the issue. Earlier He has told Laodicea, "I *know* thy works" (Revelation 3:15, emphasis supplied). He doesn't say, "I am the source of your works." He knows Laodicea's works, but He is not the source of those works. "It is your self-righteousness that you are relying on," He is telling Laodicea. "I am knocking at your heart's door in order to get your attention. I want to come in and be the source of your works, the source of your righteousness. I want to work in you from within, not from the outside. Please let Me be your righteousness, not only in terms of your standing before My Father, but in terms of your day-to-day life as well."

To understand the full significance of what Christ is saying to Laodicea, we need to remember that the New Testament divides Christians into two camps—spiritual and carnal. Paul wrote to the Christians at Corinth: "I, brethren, could not speak unto you as unto spiritual, but as unto carnal, even as unto babes in Christ" (1 Corinthians 3:1). Notice that Paul doesn't refer to these carnal Christians as the unconverted, but as "babes in Christ." Babies, as you know, don't walk perfectly at first. They fall down often as they are learning to walk. In the same way, Christian babies fall down a lot, too, as they learn to walk in the Spirit. They fall down *because* they are babies; they are weak. Paul continues, "I have fed you with milk" (verse 2). That is another problem with babies—you can't give them solid food.

Now, Paul was writing to the Christians in Corinth approximately ten years after the church had been established in that city! They were still babies in Christ, still carnal Christians; they weren't growing spiritually. In verse 3, Paul lists the problems they were continuing to have—envy, strife, divisions. These things are not the behavior of a Christian; they are the behavior of the world. But does Paul say that these carnal Christians are lost? Does he say that they are unconverted? No. In fact, in verse 16 he says, "Ye [plural] are the temple [singular] of God, and . . . the Spirit of God dwelleth in you." They *are* con-

LAODICEA

verted; they *have* experienced the new birth—but you can't tell it by their lifestyle. This is the picture of carnal Christians. Their behavior is like that of ordinary people instead of reflecting the life of the Spirit, who dwells in them.

Spiritual Christians, on the other hand, have not only been converted, but they are also walking in the Spirit. Conversion is not the factor that distinguishes carnal Christians from spiritual Christians. Both have been converted; that isn't the issue. The issue is that the spiritual Christians have learned to walk in the Spirit, and carnal Christians are still walking primarily in the flesh. Carnal Christians are still dominated by self—"self" is what the New Testament actually means by the term *flesh*. As a result, carnal Christians have a major problem: They are poor witnesses; they misrepresent Christ. When people look at them, they say, "If that is what a Christian is like, I don't want any part of it!" They are poor representatives of Christ because their behavior is so little different from that of an unconverted person.

This is the very reason the eastern European block turned to Marxism originally. The Christian church in that part of the world had lost its saltiness. All of eastern Europe had been Christian for centuries, but it was seduced into Marxism because the Christian church failed to reveal the life of Christ. And it failed to do so because, for the most part, the members of the church there were carnal Christians.

We need to recognize that carnal Christians are also in a very dangerous condition. It is very easy for the devil to pull carnal Christians away from Christ because they are already walking in the flesh. There is often very little difference between the behavior of carnal Christians and the behavior of people who are of the world. It's difficult to tell whether or not carnal Christians are converted because frequently their behavior is so similar to the way the world lives.

In contrast, spiritual Christians are not only converted; They are walking in the Spirit. Spiritual Christians live a life that is clearly different from the life worldly people live. As a result, there are two things going on in the life of spiritual Christians. First, they are subduing the flesh through the power of the Spirit. Second, they are reflecting the righteousness of Christ. Paul says, "Walk in the Spirit, and ye shall not fulfil the lust of the flesh" (Galatians 5:16). In other words, the way to conquer the flesh is not by willpower or by human effort, but by walking in the Spirit. This is the only way. "Put ye on the Lord Jesus Christ, and make not provision for the flesh, to fulfil the lusts thereof" (Romans 13:14).

So one of the evidences of spiritual Christians is that they are subduing the flesh through the power of the indwelling Spirit. The second is that they are reflecting Christ's righteousness. That is why Paul goes on to say in Galatians 5:22, 23 that when we walk in the Spirit, He produces His fruit in our lives—"love, joy, peace, longsuffering, gentleness, goodness, faith, meekness, temperance." But we need to understand that this imparted righteousness of Jesus takes place in our lives only when we have lost all confidence in the flesh, when we can say sincerely in our hearts, "Not I, but Christ."

When Christ stands outside the heart, knocking and asking us to allow Him to come in, it is this experience that He wants to accomplish in our lives. He wants us to become spiritual Christians, who walk in the Spirit and who allow Him to exhibit His fruits in our lives. He wants us to grow up spiritually so that we are no longer babies in Christ, but mature Christians.

This spiritual growth or development involves the total person—spirit, soul, and body. Paul says, "The very God of peace sanctify you wholly; and I pray God your whole spirit and soul and body be preserved blameless unto the coming of our Lord Jesus Christ" (1 Thessalonians 5:23). These three elements—spirit, soul, and body—together make up a human being. None is able to exist independently of the others. The idea of an immortal soul capable of living on without the body is a pagan Greek concept, not a biblical one. When a person dies, all three—spirit, soul, and body—come to an end. Let's

LAODICEA

look at each of these three components that together make up our humanity, from a spiritual standpoint.

The spirit. This is what Paul calls the "inner man" (Ephesians 3:16). It is the dwelling place of God. God created men and women that He might live in them. "From eternal ages it was God's purpose that every created being, from the bright and holy seraph, to man, should be a temple for the indwelling of the Creator" (*The Desire of Ages*, 161). When God created Adam, he was indwelt by the Holy Spirit. The essence of the spirit is the conscience. It is through the conscience that God convicts and directs us.

The soul. The soul is the human mind, the center of which is the will. It is in the soul that we have the power to choose and make decisions.

The body. This is the outward, visible part of our being. Because we can see the body, we can most easily grasp what it is and how it functions.

These three components of our beings have their parallels to the sanctuary of the Old Testament. Remember that the sanctuary was symbolic of Christ (see John 2:19-22) and, by extension, of believers who have become one with Christ (see 1 Corinthians 6:19). The Most Holy Place corresponds to the spirit. This is where God dwells. The Holy Place is parallel with the soul. Just as the priest functioned in the Holy Place of the earthly sanctuary, so God functions in our souls or minds. The courtyard is representative of the body. The courtyard was visible to all and was the place where sacrifice took place. Romans 12:1 tells us to present our bodies as living sacrifices to God. Incidentally, these parallels in no way negate the truth of a literal sanctuary in heaven. The Bible is clear that God lives and functions in heaven as well as in the heart of the humble believer (see Isaiah 57:15).

With this background, let's look at the spiritual growth that takes place in our entire beings when we open the door of our lives in response to Christ's knock and invite Him in. This growth involves three stages in each believer's experience: (1) the preconverted state, (2) conversion, and (3) glorification.

The preconverted state. At Creation, there was perfect harmony between the divine and the human natures. There was never a struggle in Adam between his human nature and the Holy Spirit who dwelt in him. They were in perfect harmony because Adam had been created in God's image, and God is love—*agape*. God's love, through the Holy Spirit, controlled Adam totally. His humanity reflected the glory of God, which is His selfless love.

Now, what happened when Adam sinned? When he sinned, Adam turned from being God-dependent to being self-dependent. Adam's sin was turning his back on God. The Holy Spirit left him, and he died—spiritually, not physically. Self took the place of the Holy Spirit in his life. Since all humanity was created in Adam, this is what he passed on to his posterity—to you and me. At the very heart of fallen humanity is self, or what the Bible calls our "own way" (Isaiah 53:6). God's love is selfless because *agape* never seeks its own way (see 1 Corinthians 13:5). But after the fall, sin twisted the *agape* love that was within Adam inward toward self. Since then, that is what human love has consisted of—*agape* that has taken a U-turn to focus on self. Even in our fallen condition, we possess the ability to love, but that love has become self-centered. Self-love has replaced God's divine, selfless love.

Because Adam died spiritually, his children—you and I—are also born dead spiritually. Prior to conversion, we are "dead in trespasses and sins" (Ephesians 2:1). As a result, human life came under the curse of the law. That means that Adam and his posterity no longer had any legal right to live. Humanity stood legally condemned. Further, human nature became a slave to sin, with no power to resist its demands (see Romans 5:12-21). This is the spiritual condition in which you and I and every descendant of Adam have been born. This is what the Bible means by the word *carnal*. We are born carnal; we are born domi-

LAODICEA

nated by self; we are born slaves to sin (see Romans 7:14).

To make matters even worse, there is absolutely nothing you or I can do to save ourselves from this predicament. It is as impossible as it is for an apple tree to produce oranges. The Bible is very clear on this point. "Can the Ethiopian change his skin, or the leopard his spots? Then may ye also do good, that are accustomed to do evil" (Jeremiah 13:23).

This bleak picture is our condition prior to conversion. However, to redeem us from this hopeless situation, God united Christ's divinity to our corporate humanity that needed redeeming. As the second Adam, Christ began where we begin, but by His perfect life and sacrificial death, He brought us to the place the first Adam was supposed to have brought us. This is the good news of the gospel.

Conversion. Conversion means accepting Christ by faith as our life in the place of our sinful life, which died forever on the cross (see 2 Timothy 2:11). What happens when a person is converted? What changes take place?

The first thing that happens at conversion is that the Holy Spirit, the representative of Christ (see Romans 8:9, 10), comes and dwells in our spirit. Just as the Holy Spirit dwelt in Adam before he sinned, so the Spirit dwells in us at conversion. This is because we have surrendered our lives to the cross and have accepted the formula of the gospel—"Not I, but Christ." We were spiritually dead, but now we have been made spiritually alive (see Galatians 2:20). Because we have accepted Christ as our Saviour and our righteousness, we stand justified before the law that previously condemned us. The question of whether we will be allowed into heaven is no longer an issue. As far as God is concerned, He sees the perfect history of His Son when He looks at us! We are in Christ, and God views us as perfect and complete (see Colossians 2:10).

Of course, our human nature hasn't changed one bit. It is still carnal. Our human nature is still controlled by self. Because of this, there is a conflict that takes place in the life of every converted, born-again believer. The conflict is between the divine nature, of which we have become partakers through faith and the new-birth experience, and the human nature, which is still at enmity against God. These two natures are always in conflict in the believer. Many Christians are confused about this; they think this conflict means they aren't converted. Not so! In fact, I would question your conversion if this conflict is *not* present. Before conversion, there is no conflict, because the human nature is in control. The fact that conflict is present is evidence that a new nature has been introduced. That's a good sign, because it tells us that our minds have repented and are converted, or changed. But because the sinful nature hasn't changed, conflict is inevitable (see Galatians 5:17).

Where does this conflict take place? Here is where many Christians have failed to understand the problem clearly. The battleground for the Christian is in the mind. Without the consent of our wills, the Holy Spirit cannot impart Christ's righteousness. The Spirit will never work by compulsion. Likewise, neither can the sinful nature fulfill its desires without the consent of our wills. So each is struggling for the mastery of our wills, our minds. A constant battle goes on in our minds, our thoughts, our desires. We can understand that, because we each have experienced it. I believe Romans, chapter 7 is describing this struggle that goes on after conversion. With the mind, we want to obey God's law, but the flesh wants to obey the law of sin, so the struggle is constant and severe.

When does the struggle end? It will stop only when we die or when Jesus comes. There is no way, this side of eternity, that we can say, "I have graduated from the struggle."

To put the question another way, "Can the mind ever conquer the flesh?" The answer is no. It can defy the flesh for a time, but it can never conquer it. That is because sin is a law, a constant force, residing in our members.

LAODICEA

Perhaps you have attended a Week of Prayer or a camp meeting during which you were deeply stirred spiritually. You make resolutions such as, "From now on, I am not going to eat dessert after meals!" Have you ever made that resolution?

Well, you are successful the first day and the second day and even the third day. The fourth day, you have worked very hard, and you're extremely tired. After dinner, your wife brings out some cookies she has made just for you! You look at them, and your mouth waters. You say, "Well, just this one time." Before you know what has happened, the plate is empty! The human mind, no matter how strong your will is, cannot conquer the flesh. Romans 7:15-24 makes that clear.

So the question is not, "Can the mind conquer the flesh?" The question is: "Can the Spirit conquer the flesh?" And thank God, the answer is Yes! "The law of the Spirit of life in Christ Jesus hath made me free from the law of sin and death" (Romans 8:2). In this verse, Paul is not talking about what happens in our Christian experience. He is talking about an objective truth that took place in Christ. And he is using the term *law* in the sense of a "force" or "principle," like the law of gravity. He is saying that two forces met in Christ—the law of sin and death and the law of the Spirit.

Now, where does the law of sin reside? Paul says, "I see another law in my members, warring against the law of my mind, and bringing me into captivity to the law of sin *which is in my members*" (Romans 7:23, emphasis supplied). He doesn't mean church members; he means his hands, feet, body, etc.—that is the sinful human nature. So the law of sin lives in our human nature, in the flesh. This law is not only a force, it is a constant force. The will is also a force, but it is not a constant force. Sometimes my will is strong; sometimes it is weak. That isn't true of the law of sin; it is constant all the time.

The law of the Spirit is also a constant force—like the law of sin—but it is an opposite force. One is toward sin; the other is toward righteousness.

Laodicea must open the door

This law of sin and the law of the Spirit met together in Jesus Christ—and the law of the Spirit won! "God sending his own Son in the likeness of sinful flesh, and for sin, condemned sin in the flesh" (Romans 8:3). Jesus condemned sin in the flesh for two reasons.

First, He did it to justify us. You see, it isn't only our actions that condemn us; our very natures condemn us because they are sinful. "Flesh and blood cannot inherit the kingdom of God" (1 Corinthians 15:50). On the cross, Christ not only dealt with my actions, He dealt, also, with what I am. On the cross, He executed both my sins and also the law of sin at work in my flesh. Hence, there is no condemnation for those who are in Christ (see Romans 8:1).

Second, Christ condemned sin in the flesh so that "the righteousness of the law might be fulfilled in us who walk not after the flesh, but after the Spirit" (Romans 8:4). If you walk in the Spirit, the law of the Spirit will set you free in experience from the law of sin—not to save you, but to give evidence to the world that you have been saved or justified.

So when Christ stands outside the door and knocks, when He pleads with us to open the door, He is saying, "Let Me be the source of your Christian living. Stop trying to be good; you will never succeed. I want to come in and live in you and walk in you." In other words, "I am the vine, ye are the branches. . . . Without me ye can do nothing" (John 15:5).

Christ wants Laodicea to be spiritual Christians. He is not walking in carnal Christians; therefore, carnal Christians are a misrepresentation of Christ, even though the Spirit dwells in them. The carnal Christian is one who hides his light under a bushel. The only way we can become spiritual and allow Christ to walk in us is to say, "Not I, but Christ." This is very painful to our self-righteousness, but it is the only solution to our Laodicean problem.

The unconverted person has only one life to control him—the life of the flesh. He can walk only in the flesh because that is all he has;

LAODICEA

that is all he is. But as Christians, we have two choices because we have two natures. We still have the flesh, but we also have the Spirit. So we can walk either in the flesh or in the Spirit.

Paul says, "If the Spirit of him that raised up Jesus from the dead dwell in you, he that raised up Christ from the dead shall also quicken your mortal [carnal] bodies by his Spirit that dwelleth in you" (Romans 8:11). Why does Paul bring in the resurrection of Jesus? Because that is the ultimate test. Sin's greatest power is revealed when it puts you in the grave—permanently. Have you conquered the grave? Are you immune to death—the second death? If so, then you have conquered the flesh and sin. But if not, then you still haven't conquered either sin or the flesh.

But Jesus has! Jesus has conquered the grave! He has conquered sin and the flesh! How? Was it by His own power or by the Spirit's power? Paul says here that it was by the Spirit's power that Jesus rose from the dead. So Paul is saying, "Just as the Spirit demonstrated His power over sin by raising Christ from the dead, so, also, if you are walking in the Spirit, He will be able to overcome the flesh, dead in trespasses and sins, and produce righteousness in you."

If you allow the flesh to control you, ultimately, the flesh will pull you out of Christ and down to the grave. You will die because when you walk in the flesh, you are grieving the Holy Spirit—rejecting Him and causing Him to withdraw from your life. Paul warns against this in Ephesians 4:25-30. As long as the Spirit of God dwells in you, you are sealed in terms of your eternal salvation. But it is possible to say to the Holy Spirit, "I don't want You anymore." It's possible to grieve Him to the point that He will leave you. When that happens, you are no longer under the umbrella of justification by faith. You have said goodbye to it.

So Laodicea has two possibilities. She can walk in the Spirit, or she can walk in the flesh. Both the Spirit and the flesh want control of our minds. Neither can fulfill their desires for us without our consent. So

Laodicea must open the door

there is this constant battle. I hate to tell you, but there will never come a time when your flesh will say, "I give up. I will not give you any more trouble." The flesh can be conquered, but not by you, not by your will. Only the Spirit can conquer the flesh, only as you walk in the Spirit.

In presenting the gospel to the Jews burdened under the yoke of legalism, Christ said, "Take my yoke upon you, and learn of me; . . . for my yoke is easy, and my burden is light" (Matthew 11:29, 30). Many have misunderstood this statement to mean that the Christian walk is a joint effort. That although Christ does most of the pulling, we must do our part as well. Thus, they limit righteousness by faith to justification only. For them, sanctification is a mixture of Christ's effort and human effort.

The truth is, however, that in this verse Christ was introducing a yoke that was the very opposite of what Judaism was teaching—the yoke of legalism that Paul described as a yoke of bondage (see Galatians 5:1). When Christ says, "learn of me," He wants every believer to learn that His yoke is the yoke of righteousness by faith alone—total dependence on God both for justification as well as sanctification. Just as Christ lived by the Father, so must we live by Him (see John 6:57).

That is why Jesus says to Laodicea, "Let Me come in, not only to dwell with you, but let Me eat with you as well. And you with Me. Let Me totally identify Myself with you—and you with Me." He wants to take over your life. He wants to control your spirit, your soul, your mind, your body. But He will never do so by compulsion. There is an important part for us to play—we must submit our wills to Christ's will. That is the cross. Remember Gethsemane? Jesus' flesh didn't want to die on the cross. He cried out to the Father, "Please, if there is any possible way, let this cup pass from Me! Nevertheless, not what I will, but what You will. Thy will be done."

That is what we have to say constantly. Jesus is pleading with Laodicea, "Please let Me walk in you! What you are doing may appear very nice to you, but it is polluted with self. Only when I am walking in you can the righteousness you have be true righteousness."

Are we willing to repent of our self-righteousness? Are we willing to open the door and let Christ come in and take over? Are we willing to say with Paul, "I am crucified with Christ: nevertheless I live; yet not I, but Christ liveth in me: and the life which I now live in the flesh I live by the faith of the Son of God, who loved me, and gave himself for me" (Galatians 2:20)?

When this happens, we will be good witnesses for Jesus; the world will see Him in us. And when that happens, the world will be lightened with His glory, and we will have overcome.

Glorification. This is the third stage of Christian growth. When Christ comes the second time, there will be a change—not in our minds, which are already converted, but in our natures. "This corruptible must put on incorruption, and this mortal must put on immortality" (1 Corinthians 15:53). Then the body, the soul, and the spirit will be in perfect harmony once more. The struggle will have come to an end. Divine glory will be fully restored, because the human and divine natures will again be in complete agreement. That is the glorification we look forward to when Jesus appears. Until then, you and I must groan because we have sinful flesh, which is the greatest enemy to Christian living. Nevertheless, when we open the door through genuine repentance and allow Christ to come in, we will be able to say, "I can do all things through Christ which strengtheneth me" (Philippians 4:13).

CHAPTER 9

LAODICEA
must overcome

To him that overcometh will I grant to sit with me in my throne, even as I also overcame, and am set down with my Father in his throne.
REVELATION 3:21

Earlier we saw that Christ's messages to each of the seven churches in Revelation, chapters 2 and 3 contain certain common elements. For example, to each church, Christ says, "I know thy works." These messages are Christ's evaluation of His people throughout the history of the church. He also begins His closing remarks to each church by saying, "He that overcometh . . ." followed by a promise unique to that church. The ultimate purpose of these messages to the seven churches is that God's people may be overcomers, victorious.

In what sense must Laodicea overcome? Christ tells us that He wants us to overcome, so we need to know what it is He wants us to be victorious over.

The heart of the Laodicean message, as we have seen it so far, is that we need to overcome self. Whether it is our law keeping or our good

LAODICEA

works, or whatever we take pride in, the heart of our problem as Laodicea is self-righteousness. Wherever there is self, there is sin. So the thing we need to overcome is self.

And what is Christ's promise to those in Laodicea who overcome self-righteousness? "To him that overcometh will I grant to sit with me in my throne, even as I also overcame, and am set down with my Father in his throne" (Revelation 3:21).

Christ isn't dealing here with salvation in the sense of our title to heaven. He's speaking here of a special privilege granted to those who overcome self. You see, Revelation mentions two groups of people who will be in heaven—the bride and the guests; it also distinguishes between those who serve God in His temple and everyone else who is saved (see Revelation 19:7-9; 7:15). Of course, all those who are in heaven will have received by faith the *imputed* righteousness of Jesus. There will be no one there without Christ's imputed righteousness, because that is the only thing that qualifies anyone for heaven. But I believe that those who serve God in His temple are those who have overcome self and who will sit down with Christ in His throne as He promises in Revelation 3:21. I believe that those who receive this special privilege, the bride, are the ones who appreciate Christ for what He is and who have, by faith, experienced His *imparted* righteousness, reflecting fully the self-emptying love of the Saviour.

Revelation 14 introduces us to such a group, called the 144,000:

I heard a voice from heaven, as the voice of many waters, and as the voice of a great thunder: and I heard the voice of harpers harping with their harps. And they sung as it were a new song before the throne, and before the four beasts, and the elders: and no man could learn that song but the hundred and forty and four thousand which were redeemed from the earth. These are they which were not defiled with women; for they are virgins. These are they which follow the Lamb whithersoever he goeth. These were redeemed from among men, being the firstfruits unto God and to the Lamb. And in their mouth was found no guile: for they are without fault before the throne of God (verses 2-5).

This group have not only been justified by faith, as have all believers, but they have experienced the full power of the gospel—that is, the imparted righteousness of Christ. "In their mouth was found no guile: for they are without fault before the throne of God" (verse 5). Revelation, chapter 7 also pictures this same group in these words: "These are they which came out of great tribulation, and have washed their robes, and made them white in the blood of the Lamb. Therefore are they before the throne of God, and serve him day and night in his temple; and he that sitteth on the throne shall dwell among them" (verses 14, 15). This is the privilege Christ wants to give each of us.

Christ's closing words to the Laodicean church contain something that doesn't appear in His closing words to the other six churches. To each of the six, Jesus says, "He that overcometh . . ." But He takes Laodicea one step farther; He adds, "Even as *I also overcame*" (verse 21, emphasis supplied). He wants this last generation of Christians to overcome in the same way that He overcame. The True Witness is pointing to His own victory as the example for Laodicea.

What did Christ overcome?

First, He overcame the world. He told His disciples, "In the world ye shall have tribulation: but be of good cheer; I have overcome the world" (John 16:33). What did He mean? The Bible defines the world as "the lust of the flesh, and the lust of the eyes, and the pride of life" (1 John 2:16). All this Christ overcame.

Second, He also overcame the prince of this world—Satan (see John 14:30). Jesus totally overcame Satan, and He overcame him on our behalf.

Third, He also overcame sin in the flesh. "God sending his own Son in the likeness of sinful flesh, and for sin, condemned sin in the flesh" (Romans 8:3). He condemned, or overcame, the law of sin and death—the principle of sin, which is the principle of self that dwells in sinful flesh.

All this Christ overcame—the world, the devil, and the flesh, or self—in order that He might impart this victory to you and me! He didn't overcome merely in order to give us the title and assurance of salvation. Of course, His victory does that, but He overcame also so that "that the righteousness of the law might be fulfilled in us" (verse 4).

Paul explains further what Christ has brought to us by His redemptive work. Christ "gave himself for our sins, that he might deliver us from this present evil world, according to the will of God and our Father" (Galatians 1:4). That is why we have hope. This world is not to be our home forever. We have been delivered from it, and we are also delivered from the evil that exists in this world.

The apostle John says, "Whatsoever is born of God overcometh the world: and this is the victory that overcometh the world, even our faith" (1 John 5:4). Never think that you will overcome the world and its sin by your own efforts or by your willpower. The world, the devil, and the flesh can be overcome only by faith.

Paul is quite clear in Romans, chapter 7 that in and of ourselves, we cannot keep the law or do genuine good works. He ends the chapter with a summary describing what the Christian struggle with sin is like apart from the power of the Spirit. "With the mind I myself serve the law of God; but with the flesh the law of sin" (verse 25). We can identify with Paul's lament, because we have experienced it so many times ourselves. We contend against the flesh in battle and try to overcome with the power of our converted minds. And who wins? The flesh wins! Can your mind conquer your flesh? Paul's answer in Romans, chapter 7 is No. And the answer of our experience, over and over again, is likewise No. As we saw in the previous chapter, the converted mind can defy the flesh for a time, but it can never overcome it.

Laodicea must overcome

Yet Paul goes on to say in Romans, chapter 8 that Christ has condemned—which includes overcoming—this law of sin in the flesh. And He did so in order "that the righteousness of the law might be fulfilled in us, who walk not after the flesh, but after the Spirit" (verse 4). The victory of Christ is not only to be applied to us for our benefit, but it is also for us to experience.

When Laodicea finally repents and turns from self-righteousness to the righteousness of Christ, when she walks by faith alone and no longer depends on self but on God, then all the victories described in Revelation 15 will be hers. John says:

> I saw as it were a sea of glass mingled with fire: and them that had gotten the victory over the beast, and over his image, and over his mark, and over the number of his name, stand on the sea of glass, having the harps of God. And they sing the song of Moses the servant of God, and the song of the Lamb (verses 2, 3).

The harps of God represent victory. This is God's purpose for Laodicea.

What is the secret of this victory?

John says, "Ye are of God, little children, and have overcome them [the false prophets, the antichrist, the beast, his mark, and his image] because greater is he that is in you, than he that is in the world" (1 John 4:4). John is speaking of two persons here: "he that is in you," and "he that is in the world." He that is in the world is Satan. And he that is in you is Christ's Spirit. How do we know? Paul says, "Christ in you, the hope of glory" (Colossians 1:27). And Paul adds, "For the law of the Spirit of life in Christ Jesus hath made me free from the law of sin and death" (Romans 8:2). Christ dwells in you and me through the Holy Spirit. John is saying that the Holy Spirit, who represents Christ dwelling in us, is greater than Satan, who dwells in the world. That is the source of our victory over sin.

LAODICEA

Paul presents a similar argument. He says,

> The weapons of our warfare are not carnal, but mighty through God to the pulling down of strong holds. Casting down imaginations, and every high thing that exalteth itself against the knowledge of God, and bringing into captivity every thought to the obedience of Christ (2 Corinthians 10:4, 5).

Notice what you can do in the power of "Christ in you." The Bible says it is possible to bring every thought under control by the power of the indwelling Christ.

Please be clear that these victories are not what saves us. They are the fruits of the gospel, the evidence that the power of the gospel is in us. We must never get the idea that we have to achieve these victories and overcome all these things in order to be saved. Never! Salvation is a gift to sinners. But we do have to overcome in order to sit with Christ in His throne and witness His glory.

Now comes the big question. What is the cost? What does it cost to have Christ dwelling and walking in us?

I can sum up the cost in one word—brokenness. In order to buy the heavenly merchandise offered by the True Witness—the gold purified in the fire, the white clothing, and the eye salve—we must be willing to pay the price, and the price is brokenness.

When Christ lives in us and produces His righteousness in us, only He must receive the glory. How does the flesh feel about this? It feels hurt. The flesh likes to receive glory. We love glory, don't we?

Jesus illustrated the brokenness that has to take place by what happens when we plant grain. He said, "Verily, verily, I say unto you, Except a corn of wheat fall into the ground and die, it abideth alone: but if it die, it bringeth forth much fruit" (John 12:24). The shell of a kernel of wheat is very hard. The life is not in the shell; it is inside in the germ. The shell has to be broken by water. It has to be softened

Laodicea must overcome

and broken so that the life inside may spring out and produce fruit.

Paul uses the symbol of a vase or jar. "We have this treasure in earthen vessels, that the excellency of the power may be of God, and not of us" (2 Corinthians 4:7). Mary's experience illustrates this. She came to Jesus with an alabaster jar of expensive perfume. Now, when you buy expensive perfume, it often comes in a very beautiful bottle. The bottle is so pretty that you keep the bottle even after you have used all the perfume. Mary's alabaster jar held a very expensive perfume, but it was sealed. No one knew what was in it until she broke it open. Then the smell of this expensive perfume filled the whole room.

Christ is dwelling in you and in every born-again believer. But no one can see Christ in you until the outer shell is broken. But here is the problem. We are great admirers of the beautiful bottles! We think that the church cannot do without us. Some of us feel that the church could never get along without our expertise or our academic degrees. Some of us feel that the church would collapse without our administrative abilities. Some of us feel that this church would come to nothing without our gifts.

I have to give you some bad news: None of us is indispensable. The church can survive just fine without you or me. But it cannot survive without Christ. Don't ever get the idea when Christ uses you mightily that the church cannot do without you. It is Christ in you who is the hope of glory.

For the inner Christ to shine outwardly, the shell must be broken. Self must be put aside. This world needs to see, not how good we are, which is self-righteousness, but how good Christ is. That will take place only when we are willing to be broken. Self must die in order that Christ may live in us and through us (see Philippians 3:10).

The ultimate purpose of the Laodicean message is to help us realize that God wants a people—not just individuals, but a people—through whom He can lighten the earth with His glory. When this happens, God will be able to demonstrate the power of the gospel to the world,

LAODICEA

and there will be no excuse for anyone to be lost. God will be able to say to the universe and to the disbelieving world, "Here are My people. Here are the ones who have the faith of Jesus and have overcome self as He overcame."

The devil will respond as he did in Job's case, "Let me see. Let me test them." How severe will the test be? It will be a test that no other generation has ever experienced (see Daniel 12:1; Jeremiah 30:7). When that test arrives, will Laodicea be able to overcome? God has promised that there will be a people who will overcome in His strength. The question is: Will we be willing to be broken? Will we be willing to say, "Not I, but Christ"?

The real issue is not whether we are going to heaven or not. The issue is that the world desperately needs to see Christ in us, the hope of glory. Laodicea must overcome. The stumbling block is her self-righteousness. It isn't so much that she is doing bad things; the problem is that she is doing good things for the wrong reasons. The world is waiting to see *God's* goodness, not *man's* goodness.

We have the light, but we have it under a bushel. Jesus says to us, "Ye are the light of the world. . . . Let your light so shine before men that they may see your good works *and glorify your Father which is in heaven*" (Matthew 5:14, emphasis supplied).

This isn't easy for the flesh. It means that you'll be willing to be hurt when people don't appreciate you. In the early days of missions, our pioneer missionaries faced physical hardships, wild animals, hostile tribes, and other dangers. Today, the greatest problem many missionaries face is ingratitude. The third world does not like missionaries today. To have "missionaries" come to their land implies that they are still backward.

I'll never forget my first experience as a literature evangelist in England. I knocked on the door, and when the woman opened it, I made a great mistake. I told her I was from Africa. She immediately opened my eyes. "Look," she told me, "it is we English people who have sent

Laodicea must overcome

missionaries to Africa, not the other way around." In other words, "Africa needs missionaries, but not us; we are a Christian country."

The third world feels the same today. "We don't need you; go home!" That is why so many missionaries today don't fulfill their entire term. They may sign a contract for six years, but most of them come home before the six years are up. And one of the main reasons is that the people they are trying to help don't appreciate them. Our church members in these countries appreciate what is being done, but the people of the country as a whole and the government officials don't like having missionaries in their country.

Are we willing to swallow our pride when that attitude occurs? Are we willing to be hurt even by a fellow church member and not give up? Ellen White says that we are to draw warmth from the coldness of others in these last days (see *Testimonies for the Church*, 5:136).

When someone says something that hurts you, please don't say, "I'll quit coming to church." Jesus wasn't appreciated either when He arrived in our world. "He came unto his own, and his own received him not" (John 1:11). What would have happened to us if Jesus had said, "These people don't appreciate the tremendous sacrifice I'm making for them. I'll go back to heaven"?

Christ didn't let ingratitude or abuse deter Him from His mission. They spit on Him and made fun of Him. Have you ever been spit on? And what was Jesus' response? "Father, forgive them." In spite of the way the world treated Him, Jesus hung on and overcame. He overcame pride. He overcame self. He was obedient even to the death of the cross; He was willing to empty Himself and become nothing so that you and I might be in His kingdom!

When Laodicea—you and I—are willing to surrender self and let the Holy Spirit take over, then we will overcome. Then the world will be lightened by God's glory. We need to begin today in our neighborhood, in our own church. But we don't overcome by trying harder. "This is the victory that overcometh the world, even our faith" (1 John 5:4).

CHAPTER 10

LAODICEA
is sealed

I saw four angels standing on the four corners of the earth, holding the four winds of the earth, that the wind should not blow on the earth, nor on the sea, nor on any tree. And I saw another angel ascending from the east, having the seal of the living God: and he cried with a loud voice to the four angels, to whom it was given to hurt the earth and the sea, saying, Hurt not the earth, neither the sea, nor the trees, till we have sealed the servants of our God in their foreheads.
REVELATION 7:1-3

In this chapter and the next, we will shift our attention away from Christ's specific message to Laodicea in Revelation, chapter 3 to other passages in Revelation that have implications for Laodicea. Keep in mind that although Christ appeals to each of the other six churches to overcome, He appeals to Laodicea to overcome *as He overcame*.

Since Laodicea represents the last generation of Christians, it must

LAODICEA

include those who will face the final showdown in the great controversy between Christ and Satan. Revelation identifies this final crisis as Armageddon.

> I saw three unclean spirits like frogs come out of the mouth of the dragon, and out of the mouth of the beast, and out of the mouth of the false prophet. For they are the spirits of devils, working miracles, which go forth unto the kings of the earth and of the whole world, to gather them to the battle of that great day of God Almighty. Behold, I come as a thief. Blessed is he that watcheth, and keepeth his garments, lest he walk naked, and they see his shame. And he gathered them together into a place called in the Hebrew tongue Armageddon (Revelation 16:13-16).

These three unclean spirits might be said to be the counterparts to the three angel messengers of Revelation, chapter 14. The three angels bring God's messages and prepare a people for the end time. In contrast, the three unclean spirits are agents of Satan to prepare the world for the time of trouble and for the final conflict between good and evil.

Please note that Armageddon is described as "the battle of that great day of God Almighty" (verse 14). It is not a Middle East crisis; it has nothing to do with the Middle East. It is the final conflict between God and Satan, between God's people (the church) and Satan's followers (the world). Verse 15 indicates that this battle will take place just before Jesus returns.

This verse is also a clear link with Christ's message to Laodicea. Jesus offers Laodicea "white raiment, that thou mayest be clothed, and that the shame of thy nakedness do not appear" (Revelation 3:18). Revelation 16:15 says, "Blessed is he that watcheth, and keepeth his garments [Christ's righteousness], lest he walk naked, and they see his shame." We are to hold on to the righteousness of Christ by faith

Laodicea is sealed

right up to the very end.

From the Christian's viewpoint, Armageddon is the "great tribulation," in which God's people will be tested in a way that no previous generation has experienced. Two Old Testament passages describe this great tribulation—one in Daniel and one in Jeremiah. Daniel says that when the ministry of Christ is finished in the heavenly sanctuary,

> At that time shall Michael stand up, the great prince which standeth for the children of thy people: and there shall be a time of trouble such as never was since there was a nation even to that same time: and at that time thy people shall be delivered, every one that shall be found written in the book (Daniel 12:1).

Jeremiah's description is similar:

> Alas! for that day is great, so that none is like it: it is even the time of Jacob's trouble; but he shall be saved out of it (Jeremiah 30:7).

What will the real issue be in this time of trouble? What is it that we Laodiceans need to overcome in order to successfully meet this great final conflict?

I believe that in this great tribulation God's people will have to reproduce Jesus' victory on the cross. Three times, Satan tempted Jesus to come down from the cross and save Himself—once through the Roman soldiers, once through the Jewish priests, and once through the thief at His left side (see Luke 23:35-39). Using His divine power, independently of the Father, Christ could have left the cross and saved Himself. But He didn't; He hung on the cross and faced this last terrible temptation. Here is how Ellen White describes it:

> Amid the awful darkness, apparently forsaken of God, Christ

LAODICEA

had drained the last dregs in the cup of human woe. In those dreadful hours He had relied upon the evidence of His Father's acceptance heretofore given Him. He was acquainted with the character of His Father; He understood His justice, His mercy, and His great love. By faith He rested in Him whom it had ever been His joy to obey. And as in submission He committed Himself to God, the sense of the loss of His Father's favor was withdrawn. By faith, Christ was victor (*The Desire of Ages*, 756).

Notice that it was *by faith*, not feeling, that Christ overcame. His feelings told Him that the Father had forsaken Him, but by faith He believed God would never do so. By faith, Jesus was victorious. In the same way, during the time of trouble, our faith will be tested to the limit. We will *feel* abandoned by God Himself. We will *feel* that we are without hope. But by *faith* we will cling to God's promises and overcome. Those whose faith endures are known in Revelation as the 144,000. These are those in Laodicea who overcome even as Christ overcame.

Isaiah gives us insight into the issues in this time of trouble. God says through Isaiah, "For a small moment have I forsaken thee; but with great mercies will I gather thee. In a little wrath I hid my face from thee for a moment; but with everlasting kindness will I have mercy on thee, saith the Lord thy Redeemer" (Isaiah 54:7, 8). We will feel apparently forsaken by God during the great tribulation.

In this final showdown, God will say, "Here are My people, who have the faith of Jesus Christ."

And the devil will challenge Him. "Give them into my hands," he will demand. "Let's see how faithful they will be."

God replies, "You can touch them, you can do anything you like with them, but you cannot kill them." We will be at the mercy of the world, which will be fully controlled by Satan.

Will there be a people whose faith, like that of Jesus on the cross,

Laodicea is sealed

will endure to the very end (see Luke 18:8)? That is the question. And the good news is that the answer is Yes! They are called the 144,000 and are pictured in only two passages in the entire New Testament—Revelation, chapters 7 and 14.

Revelation 7 is answering the question asked in the last verse of chapter 6: "The great day of his [the Lamb's] wrath is come; and who shall be able to stand?" (verse 17). In context, this question is especially pertinent. Chapter 6 has pictured the great second coming of Jesus with cataclysmic upheavals in nature and wholesale panic seemingly by everyone on earth—the rich, the poor, the free, the slaves, kings, and mighty men. They are all crying for the rocks and mountains to fall on them and hide them from the Lamb on His throne (see verses 12-16). No one, it seems, is able to stand the second coming of Christ. So verse 17 asks the question, "Who is able to stand? Is anyone able?"

Will God be able to produce a people who have reproduced in their lives Christ's victory on the cross?

The answer is found in Revelation, chapter 7, and the answer is Yes! God will have such a people. Verse 1 pictures four angels holding back the four winds that are about to blow on the earth and the sea and the trees. Winds, of course, symbolize strife and war. At the end time, God says to Satan, "Here are My people."

And Satan says, "Give them into my hands and let me test them."

But God says, "Not yet. I will protect My people and hold back the strife, the great tribulation. I will hold it until we have sealed them."

What does the sealing mean?

In Romans, chapter 4, Paul gives us an example of its meaning. He argues with the Jewish Christians in Rome that circumcision does not contribute in the least to salvation. But he anticipates a question that the Jews in Rome will ask him, "If circumcision has no significance for our salvation, why did God give it to Abraham and to his descendants?"

And Paul's reply is that Abraham "received the sign of circumcision,

LAODICEA

a seal of the righteousness of the faith which he had yet being uncircumcised" (verse 11).

Abraham had righteousness by faith long before he was circumcised. Circumcision didn't contribute anything to his righteousness; it did something else, Paul says. It sealed what Abraham already had. It confirmed, or authenticated, the righteousness he already possessed. This is important because I believe that the seal of God in the last days is not circumcision, but the Sabbath. Like circumcision, Sabbath keeping does not make us righteous; it does not contribute anything to our salvation. It only seals something that is already there. The significance of circumcision and of the Sabbath are synonymous in this regard. Both are signs of an experience—righteousness by faith.

So the sealing of God's people in the last days simply means that their faith in the Lord of the Sabbath has become unshakable. They have settled into the truth of Jesus Christ our righteousness. They have purchased the white raiment from Christ and have made that their only hope. There is no turning back to self. They have come to understand God's character, His love and His mercy, and His finished work of redemption so clearly that their faith is unchangeably resting in Him. That is the sealing, and the Sabbath is only the sign of that experience.

Exodus, chapter 31 gives us evidence that God designed the Sabbath to be a sign, or seal, of an experience. "Verily my sabbaths ye shall keep: for it is a sign between me and you throughout your generations; that ye may know that I am the Lord that doth sanctify you" (Exodus 31:13). And Hebrews 10:14 tells us that we were perfected by one sacrifice—the cross.

God's people are sealed in their foreheads, indicating that they have the mind of Christ. The mind of Christ was an attitude that was totally emptied of self. When God's people are sealed, there will be no more wavering. It is in this context that Christ will say, "He that is unjust, let him be unjust still: and he which is filthy, let him be filthy

Laodicea is sealed

still: and he that is righteous, let him be righteous still: and he that is holy, let him be holy still" (Revelation 22:11). Those in both camps—God's people and Satan's followers—have made up their minds irrevocably and therefore have been sealed. Satan's followers are sealed with the mark of the beast, and God's people are sealed with the seal of God.

Jesus was sealed in Gethsemane. It was there that He made up His mind beyond any changing. He struggled there in the garden until He could say, "Not my will, but thine, be done." And at Calvary, He carried out the decision of that sealing experience. Like Him, we will be sealed before the great time of trouble. That tribulation will test whether our faith is unshakable, and we will overcome even as He overcame.

The Bible pictures those who are sealed as the 144,000. Is this a literal number? Will God's people who are sealed actually number 144,000?

We have argued endlessly over this question in the church. I can only give you what I believe to be true. You can accept it or not. In Revelation, chapter 7, John says, "I heard the number of them which were sealed: and there were sealed an hundred and forty and four thousand of all the tribes of the children of Israel" (verse 4). Now, we can understand this verse to be literal or figurative. But it seems to me that if we are going to interpret the number as literal, then we need to interpret the entire verse as literal. John says that those who were sealed were from the twelve tribes of Israel (see verse 4). If this is to be interpreted literally, then there is no hope that we Gentiles can be among the 144,000 who are sealed.

On the other hand, if the number is symbolic, then the rest of the verse can be interpreted symbolically as well. In general, how does the New Testament interpret the idea of Israel?

In his letter to the Roman Christians, Paul argues that "Israel" does not mean only those who are physically descended from Abraham, but

LAODICEA

all those who have accepted Christ—whether or not they are Abraham's physical descendants. "For they are not all Israel, which are of Israel. Neither, because they are the seed of Abraham, are they all children: but, In Isaac shall thy seed be called. That is, They which are the children of the flesh, these are not the children of God: but the children of the promise are counted for the seed" (Romans 9:6-8).

Paul is saying that just as Isaac was Abraham's son as the result of a divine promise and a divine miracle, so all those who have accepted the divine promise and miracle of the new birth are Abraham's children—not just those who are physically Israel.

The Jews, or Israelites, looked to three great ancestors—Abraham, Isaac, and Jacob. Abraham's outstanding characteristic was his faith; he stands for faith. Isaac, because of the miracle of his birth, represents the new-birth experience. Jacob was the one who endured to the end. That is why the time of trouble is also called the time of Jacob's trouble—because Jacob persevered to the end and prevailed. All those who, like Abraham, have an unshakable faith; all those who, like Isaac, experience the new birth; all those who, like Jacob, endure to the end—these belong to Christ and are therefore "Abraham's seed, and heirs according to the promise" (Galatians 3:29).

This is how the New Testament interprets Israel—symbolically and not literally. Therefore, I believe that the number of 144,000 is also symbolic and that it refers to an indeterminate number of those, Jews and Gentiles alike, who have experienced the full power of the gospel and are reflecting Christ completely. But before God removes His protection and allows Satan to initiate the great war of Armageddon, God's people must be sealed.

There is another indication that the number 144,000 is not intended to be understood literally. In some Bible manuscripts, the text of Revelation 7:4 does not read "144,000" as you see it in your English Bible. In some manuscripts it is given as "one hundred forty-four and 1,000"—the 144 is written out in words, and the 1,000 is written in numbers. It

Laodicea is sealed

is a very strange way of writing, which seems to indicate a distinction of some kind between the two parts of the number. I've struggled to understand what this might mean. Perhaps this way of writing the number is intended to indicate that the symbol of 144,000 represents a perfect number, since it is a combination of the perfect church (12 tribes of Israel x 12 = 144) and the final work of Christ in the Most Holy Place of the heavenly sanctuary, the measurements of which are 10 cubits x 10 cubits x 10 cubits = 1,000.

Notice, too, that John doesn't *see* those who are sealed; he only *hears* the number (see verse 4). I believe John didn't see this group, because they are not located in one place; they are scattered all over the world. The 144,000 are not just in the Middle East; they are all over the world. Likewise, the battle of Armageddon is not localized to a single place in the Middle East; it is a worldwide conflict between Christ and Satan. But after the 144,000 have gone through the great tribulation and have experienced the second coming of Christ, then John *sees* them. "After this I beheld, and, lo, a great multitude, which no man could number, of all nations, and kindreds, and people, and tongues, stood before the throne, and before the Lamb, clothed in white robes, and palms in their hands" (verse 9).

Many feel that verse 9 refers not to the 144,000 but to the great multitude of all generations who will be saved from the earth. Others believe that this is the great multitude who have been converted by the 144,000. I believe, however, that this great multitude John sees in verse 9 are the 144,000. Again, this is my personal opinion, but here is why I believe it is true:

1. The context of Revelation, chapter 7 is dealing only with the 144,000—those who are able to stand during the great time of trouble and when Jesus comes.

2. This great multitude are clothed in white with palm branches in their hands. According to Revelation 19:7, 8, the white robes represent the imparted righteousness of Christ—something this last gen-

eration of Christians will experience to the full.

3. Revelation 7:14 indicates that this great multitude are those who have come "out of great tribulation and have washed their robes, and made them white in the blood of the Lamb." They have experienced total victory; they have overcome as Christ overcame. This can refer only to the 144,000.

Reflecting Christ's promise to Laodicea that those who overcame as He has overcome will sit with Him in His throne, John goes on to say of this great multitude, "Therefore are they before the throne of God, and serve him day and night in his temple: and he that sitteth on the throne shall dwell among them. They shall hunger no more, neither thirst any more; neither shall the sun light on them, nor any heat. For the Lamb which is in the midst of the throne shall feed them, and shall lead them unto living fountains of waters: and God shall wipe away all tears from their eyes" (verses 15-17). They will never go through the great tribulation again. They have been delivered out of it. I believe that God will seal a great multitude in the last days—not merely 144,000.

The gospel is the power of God unto salvation, and it is stronger by far than all the power Satan can muster through the flesh. I believe the gospel will produce not merely 144,000 faithful Christians in the last days, but a vast multitude who will refuse to compromise their faith. If what happened at Pentecost is a foretaste of what the gospel's power will accomplish at the end of time, when the fourth angel descends to lighten the entire earth with God's glory, can we imagine the transformation that will take place? Pentecost affected only a small area. What will happen when God pours out His Spirit on the whole earth? The three angels' messages, the everlasting gospel, righteousness by faith in verity—this is what will usher in these tremendous scenes of God's glory and power.

The time of trouble will be terrible. Our imaginations cannot begin to conjure up how terrible it will be. Normally, our imagination mag-

Laodicea is sealed

nifies potential problems, and reality is much less severe. But in this case, that will not be so. The only indication we have of the severity of the trials that we will face then is the tribulation Christ experienced on the cross. Like Christ, we will feel forsaken of God. The devil will take advantage of these feelings to whisper, "Do you know why God has forsaken you? Because you are lost. He has abandoned you because there is no hope of salvation for you."

And your feelings will confirm what Satan is saying. Your feelings will tell you that there is no hope for you. Yet your faith will say, "I believe Jesus. He has said, 'I will never leave you or forsake you.' My righteousness is not in me, but in Jesus Christ. I will trust Him though the heavens fall."

The real issue during the time of Jacob's trouble will be righteousness by faith—not sinless living. We won't be conscious of living sinlessly. The great issue will be: Are you willing to rest in Christ, the Lord of the Sabbath, even though you feel forsaken by God and undeserving of heaven?

Because your faith is sealed, you will survive this great tribulation. The devil will do his best to unsettle your faith, and when he fails, then he will pass a death decree against God's people. This is going beyond the limits God has agreed to. As He did with Job, God has told Satan that he cannot kill His faithful people. Then the end will come; a great earthquake will take place, and God's people will come out of their hiding places as they see their Saviour descending from heaven with thousands and thousands of His holy angels. "Look," we will shout, "it is Jesus, whom we have been waiting for!"

Those who have been threatening us and trying to kill us will run into the vacated caves and cry out to the rocks and mountains to fall on them and hide them from the consuming glory of Jesus. They can't bear the sight; they would prefer their lives be crushed out in the great earthquake!

Yes, God will have a faithful people who will overcome just as the

LAODICEA

Saviour has overcome—by faith. We need to overcome unbelief. That is Laodicea's greatest need. We need to buy the white clothing, the pure gold, the eye salve. We need to stop looking at self for assurance; we need to stop looking at our own experience. We need to rest in Christ and His righteousness. Our part, from beginning to end, is faith. Maintaining faith is our greatest struggle because, by nature, we are self-dependent.

A time of trouble is coming, but God will give us victory. May Christ make our faith so strong that we will have not only faith *in* Jesus Christ, but the faith *of* Jesus Christ.

CHAPTER 11

LAODICEA
is faultless

I looked, and, lo, a Lamb stood on the mount Sion, and with him an hundred forty and four thousand, having his Father's name written in their foreheads. . . . And they sung as it were a new song before the throne, . . . and no man could learn that song but the hundred and forty and four thousand, which were redeemed from the earth. These are they which were not defiled with women; for they are virgins. These are they which follow the Lamb whithersoever he goeth. These were redeemed from among men, being the firstfruits unto God and to the Lamb. And in their mouth was found no guile: for they are without fault before the throne of God.
REVELATION 14:1-5

In the previous chapter, we looked at Revelation, chapter 7, the first of the two New Testament passages that deal with the 144,000. We saw that Revelation, chapter 7 discusses the 144,000 in the context of the question "Who will be able to stand during the

LAODICEA

great tribulation that will precede the second coming of Christ in all His glory?"

Revelation, chapter 14, the second passage dealing with the 144,000, describes their spiritual attainments or qualities. It presents this faultless group in the setting of the three angels' messages, which are themselves the message of Christ our righteousness. It is the proclamation and acceptance of this message—righteousness by faith—that will produce the 144,000.

Thus, the three angels' messages can be described as a sealing message. They prepare a people for the last days and the coming of Jesus. The three angels' messages are also God's final call to a doomed world to accept His Son, Jesus Christ, as their only hope of salvation.

Notice how Revelation, chapter 14 begins: "I looked . . ." (verse 1). Remember that in chapter 7, John *hears* the 144,000 when they are scattered over the earth; he doesn't see them until they are gathered in heaven. Now, in chapter 14, he sees them. Chapter 14 is dealing with the 144,000 after they have arrived in heaven. This seems evident from the statements that follow. The Lamb is on Mt. Zion with the 144,000 around Him (see verse 1).

Mention is made, again, of the fact that the 144,000 are sealed, having the name of God written in their foreheads. Chapter 14 contrasts God's seal with the mark of the beast (see verses 1, 9). Both God's people and Satan's followers receive a seal or mark in their foreheads—either God's seal or the mark of the beast. When the three angels' messages have been proclaimed to the whole world as a witness, when the subject of Christ our righteousness has swallowed up every other issue, then the entire human race will be divided into just two camps. No one will be left sitting on the fence. As Christ once said, "He that is not with me is against me" (Matthew 12:30). Then there will be only believers and unbelievers.

Those who have accepted Christ's righteousness will have surrendered themselves to His cross. They will say, "I am crucified with Christ:

Laodicea is faultless

nevertheless I live; yet not I, but Christ liveth in me: and the life which I now live in the flesh I live by the faith of the Son of God, who loved me, and gave himself for me" (Galatians 2:20). Those in Satan's camp will cry out, "Crucify Him!"

Like Revelation, chapter 7, chapter 14 also pictures the 144,000 as a great multitude. After he sees the 144,000 standing with the Lamb on Mt. Zion, John says, "I heard a voice from heaven, as the voice of many waters, and as the voice of a great thunder" (verse 2). The Greek words translated "many waters" actually mean "rushing waters." It sounded like thunder to John's ears.

In Africa, we have flash floods. It rains tremendous amounts of water in a short time, and many of the roads have no bridges. When these flash floods come, the sound of rushing water is like thunder. You can hear the water rushing along, and before you know it, everything is swept away. That is how John describes the voice of the 144,000. He hears the sound of a huge multitude, numberless people, and it sounds like the thunder of a rushing flood of water. This verse is not referring to all the saved in general, but to the 144,000, since verse 3 goes on to say that only they can sing the new song that no one but the 144,000 can learn. Why is it that only the 144,000 can sing this song? It is because this song describes their experience of complete trust in Jesus as their righteousness.

Verses 4 and 5 describe the spiritual characteristics of the 144,000. They are spiritually pure (have not been defiled with women). The contrast is between this group and God's enemies, who are in Babylon, the mother of harlots (see Revelation 17:5). Babylon is also characterized by self. Nebuchadnezzar exalted himself, saying, "Look at this great city that I have built." In contrast, the 144,000 have lost all confidence in the flesh; they are rejoicing in Christ.

Verse 4 also says that the 144,000 are "virgins." I once had a church member come to me and say, "You know, no married person can be among the 144,000 because the Bible says they must be virgins." That

LAODICEA

is the problem with interpreting everything literally. We must always remember that Revelation is written in symbolic terms. The 144,000 are virgins in the same sense that Paul was talking about when he wrote to the Corinthian Christians, "I have espoused you [engaged you] to one husband, that I may present you as a chaste virgin to Christ" (2 Corinthians 11:2). He continues, "But I fear, lest by any means . . .your minds should be corrupted from the simplicity that is in Christ" (verse 3). Paul is saying, "I want you to be totally grounded in Christ and in His gospel; I want you to be trusting completely in the righteousness that is in Christ. I want to present you to Christ as a virgin, undefiled by self, but I'm afraid that you will be easily swept away from the gospel."

So when John says that the 144,000 are virgins and have not been defiled by women, he is saying that they are no longer defiled by self or any human substitute for the pure righteousness of Christ. They are resting in Him as their only Saviour, their only hope.

John also says that the 144,000 will "follow the Lamb whithersoever he goeth" (Revelation 14:4). The term *Lamb* is used of Christ in the context of sacrifice. Jesus said, "If any man will come after me [follow me], let him deny himself, and take up his cross daily, and follow me" (Luke 9:23). Those who follow the Lamb wherever He goes will share in His cross.

The cross is not just a piece of wood on which Jesus died. It is a truth; it is the truth of God's verdict of death to the flesh or human nature; it is a symbol of death to self. "They that are Christ's have crucified the flesh with the affections and lusts" (Galatians 5:24).

In each believer, there are two natures struggling for supremacy. There is the flesh, which is our natural, sinful life. And there is the Spirit, which is the divine nature of which every born-again believer has become a partaker. These two natures can never be at peace, can never come to a partnership or marriage. The moment we try to combine these two, we are committing spiritual fornication. The flesh and

Laodicea is faultless

the Spirit are implacable enemies (see Romans 8:5; Galatians 5:16, 17).

What the flesh sees, the flesh wants. At the very center of the flesh is self. The self covets everything. We need to realize that our sinful, human nature will never be satisfied until it takes over the place of God. If God didn't put restrictions on the flesh, it would end up getting rid of anything or anyone who stands in its way. To reach its ultimate goal, the flesh even has to get rid of God, because its ultimate goal is to take God's place.

All this is revealed by the cross of Christ. It revealed that sin, if given free reign, would end up crucifying the Son of God Himself. That is why we cannot take sin lightly. Sin is far more than simply breaking a rule or doing something bad. Sin is essentially self taking the place of God. Sin is saying, "I, not Christ."

When the Spirit says No to the flesh, the flesh is not happy; it suffers. All through His life on earth, from His birth to the cross, Jesus stood on the platform of "Not My will, but God's will be done." All His earthly life, the flesh suffered, and God's will was performed in Him (see 1 Peter 4:1). In Revelation, chapter 14 we see a group of people, the 144,000, who are willing to take the same stand and suffer as Christ did.

The 144,000 are described as those who have been "redeemed from among men, being the firstfruits unto God and to the Lamb" (Revelation 14:4). One significance of the term *firstfruits* is that it means the harvesttime has arrived. In this same chapter, after the three angels' messages have produced the 144,000, John sees a harvest scene. Christ sits on a cloud holding a sharp sickle. An angel comes out of the temple in heaven and cries, "Thrust in thy sickle, and reap: for the time is come for thee to reap; for the harvest of the earth is ripe" (verse 15). As the firstfruits, the 144,000 are a sign that the harvest is just around the corner.

The firstfruits also symbolize the fruit or grain that ripens first and

LAODICEA

reaches maturity before the rest of the crop. Even though the 144,000 are the last generation of Christians in point of time, they are the first ones to reach spiritual maturity in Christ. All believers will grow up spiritually and mature in heaven. But the 144,000 will reach spiritual maturity here on earth just before Jesus comes.

In the Bible, our English word *perfect* often translates the original word meaning "maturity." For example, in Matthew, chapter 5, Jesus contrasts egocentric human love with God's *agape* love. He says, "Ye have heard that it hath been said, Thou shalt love thy neighbour, and hate thine enemy" (verse 43). This was the kind of love taught by the scribes and Pharisees. But Jesus goes on to say that a person doesn't even need to be a Christian to practice this level of love; even sinners do this. Jesus presents a higher standard of love. "But I say unto you, Love your enemies, bless them that curse you, do good to them that hate you, and pray for them which despitefully use you, and persecute you" (verse 44). He concludes, "Be ye therefore perfect [mature], even as your Father which is in heaven is perfect" (verse 48).

Loving unconditionally, loving those who are unlovable, this is spiritual perfection, spiritual maturity. This is the way God loves—unconditionally. This is the way Jesus loved those who mistreated Him. When they cursed Him on the cross, He prayed for their forgiveness. He showed only love for those who hated Him. To love as He loved is to be one with Him.

When Christ said we must be perfect, or mature, as His Father in heaven is perfect, He meant that we must love unconditionally, spontaneously, whether or not the object of that love treats us well or badly. We must love others as God loves us.

The 144,000 will fully reflect this unconditional love of God. This is perfection, spiritual maturity, because love is the fulfilling of the law (see Romans 13:10; Galatians 5:14). It is in this sense that Jesus will say, "Here are they that keep the commandments of God" (Revelation 14:12).

We must be clear about what Jesus means when He speaks of our keeping the commandments. Does He mean in the letter, or does He mean in the spirit? The Jews were experts at keeping the letter of the law. So are many Seventh-day Adventists. But is that what Christ is looking for? The letter of the law is important, but more important is the spirit of the law. We can keep the letter of the law and be totally out of harmony with its spirit or intent. But if we are keeping the spirit of the law, we will be in harmony with the letter of the law as well.

So when the 144,000 are called the "firstfruits" of those who are redeemed, it means that (1) they are the first to reach full spiritual maturity; (2) they are the sign that the harvest of the earth is ripe; and (3) they are the prototype of what others will be.

The 144,000 will manifest the full power of the gospel while still living on this earth. In heaven, all believers, all the saved, will reflect the character of Christ. But not all will have reached that maturity while still living on earth. The fact that the 144,000 do so is the greatest evidence of the power of the gospel over sin and self.

In describing the 144,000 further, John says, "In their mouth was found no guile" (Revelation 14:5). Peter uses the same expression in describing Christ's behavior at the cross:

> Christ also suffered for us, leaving us an example, that ye should follow his steps. Who did no sin, *neither was guile found in his mouth.* Who, when he was reviled, reviled not again; when he suffered, he threatened not; but committed himself to him that judgeth righteously. Who his own self bare our sins in his own body on the tree, that we, being dead to sins, should live unto righteousness: by whose stripes ye were healed (1 Peter 2:21-24, emphasis supplied).

Christ was willing to suffer that we should be saved. We must be willing to suffer that He might be glorified. That is what the 144,000

LAODICEA

are willing to do. Will they be persecuted in the great tribulation? Will they be mistreated? Will they be reviled? Will they suffer? Yes, they will face all these situations. How will they react? They will react as Christ did. They will keep quiet; they will not fight back. They have no guile in their mouths. This is the power of the gospel. The greatest test that will come to us during the great time of trouble is this: Will we be willing to say goodbye to salvation and heaven itself in order that Christ might be glorified in us? That is what He was willing to do for us. Will we, by faith, overcome even as He overcame?

That is the test. I know of two individuals who have successfully passed it and who, I believe, will also receive the privilege of being among the 144,000. One is Moses, who was willing to be erased from God's Book of Life so that the rebellious Israelites, who had given him such a difficult time, could be in heaven (see Exodus 32:32). The other is Paul, who was willing to be cursed himself and lose eternal life in order that his fellow Jews might be saved (see Romans 9:1-3).

Can the gospel produce such a people—not merely one or two individuals, but a church of such people, who will lighten the earth with God's glory?

The answer is Yes. The three angels' messages, which are righteousness by faith in verity, will do it. That is the only thing that can produce such an experience—a clear understanding of Christ's righteousness and a heart response to it.

Finally, John says that the 144,000 are "without fault before the throne of God" (Revelation 14:5). Revelation 7:14 says they "have washed their robes and made them white in the blood of the Lamb." This is how they are without fault. They stand in the perfect righteousness of Jesus, imparted to them by faith. "Here are they that keep the commandments of God, and the faith of Jesus" (Revelation 14:12).

So here we have a picture of a people, the 144,000, who are cleansed, who fully reflect the character of Christ, who are undefiled and without fault. How will this happen?

Laodicea is faultless

Will it happen as a result of promotional programs? By incentives? By skillful administration? No. It will come about only through the preaching of the gospel, by the righteousness of Christ as presented in the messages of the three angels, and by our response to these messages in faith. Christ and His righteousness is the only truth that can produce such a people.

God has a great plan for Laodicea—this last generation of Christians. The proclamation of the three angels' messages will bring that plan to fruition. It will produce a people who will be able to stand in the great tribulation and at the second coming of Jesus. Remember that in His divinity, Christ is a consuming fire. Anyone not covered by His righteousness will be consumed at the second coming. But the 144,000 will be able to stand that consuming glory, not because they are good in themselves, but because they are clothed with the white raiment—the righteousness of Christ. In joy, they will cry out, "This is our God and Saviour; we have been waiting patiently for Him, and here He is!"

"The Spirit and the bride say, Come. And let him that heareth say, Come. And let him that is athirst come. And whosoever will, let him take the water of life freely" (Revelation 22:17).

"He which testifieth these things saith, Surely I come quickly. Amen. Even so, come, Lord Jesus" (verse 20).